AAT

Q2022

Internal Accounting Systems and Controls (INAC)

EXAM KIT

This Study Text supports study for the following AAT qualifications:

AAT Level 4 Diploma in Professional Accounting

AAT Diploma in Professional Accounting at SCQF Level 8

KAPLAN

PUBLISHING

British Library Cataloguing-in-Publication Data

A catalogue record for this book is available from the British Library.

Published by:

Kaplan Publishing UK

Unit 2 The Business Centre

Molly Millar's Lane

Wokingham

Berkshire

RG41 2QZ

ISBN: 978-1-83996-065-9

Kaplan Publishing are constantly finding new ways to support students looking for exam success and our online resources really do add an extra dimension to your studies.

This book comes with free MyKaplan online resources so that you can study anytime, anywhere. **This free online resource is not sold separately and is included in the price of the book.**

Having purchased this book, you have access to the following online study materials:

CONTENT	AAT	
	Text	Kit
Electronic version of the book	✓	✓
Knowledge Check tests with instant answers	✓	
Mock assessments online	✓	✓
Material updates	✓	✓

How to access your online resources

Kaplan Financial students will already have a MyKaplan account and these extra resources will be available to you online. You do not need to register again, as this process was completed when you enrolled. If you are having problems accessing online materials, please ask your course administrator.

If you are not studying with Kaplan and did not purchase your book via a Kaplan website, to unlock your extra online resources please go to www.mykaplan.co.uk/add-online-resources (even if you have set up an account and registered books previously). You will then need to enter the ISBN number (on the title page and back cover) and the unique pass key number contained in the scratch panel below to gain access. You will also be required to enter additional information during this process to set up or confirm your account details.

If you purchased through the Kaplan Publishing website you will automatically receive an e-mail invitation to MyKaplan. Please register your details using this email to gain access to your content. If you do not receive the e-mail or book content, please contact Kaplan Publishing.

Your Code and Information

This code can only be used once for the registration of one book online. This registration and your online content will expire when the final sittings for the examinations covered by this book have taken place. Please allow one hour from the time you submit your book details for us to process your request.

Please scratch the film to access your unique code.

Please be aware that this code is case-sensitive and you will need to include the dashes within the passcode, but not when entering the ISBN.

CONTENTS

Features in this revision kit

In addition to providing a wide ranging bank of real exam style questions, we have also included in this kit:

- Paper specific information and advice on exam technique.

- Our recommended approach to make your revision for this particular subject as effective as possible.

You will find a wealth of other resources to help you with your studies on the AAT website:

www.aat.org.uk/

Quality and accuracy are of the utmost importance to us so if you spot an error in any of our products, please send an email to mykaplanreporting@kaplan.com with full details.

Our Quality Co-ordinator will work with our technical team to verify the error and take action to ensure it is corrected in future editions.

UNIT SPECIFIC INFORMATION

THE EXAM

FORMAT OF THE ASSESSMENT

The assessment is divided into several standalone tasks which cover all of the learning outcomes and assessment criteria.

In any one assessment, students may not be assessed on all content, or on the full depth or breadth of a piece of content. The content assessed may change over time to ensure validity of assessment, but all assessment criteria will be tested over time.

The learning outcomes for this unit are as follows:

	Learning outcome	Weighting
1	Understand the role and responsibilities of the accounting function within an organisation	10%
2	Evaluate internal control systems	25%
3	Evaluate an organisation's accounting system and underpinning procedures	25%
4	Understand the impact of technology on accounting systems	15%
5	Recommend improvements to an organisation's accounting system	25%
	Total	100%

Time allowed

2 hours 30 minutes

PASS MARK

The pass mark is 70

 Always keep your eye on the clock and make sure you attempt all questions!

DETAILED SYLLABUS

The detailed syllabus and study guide written by the AAT can be found at:

www.aat.org.uk/

KAPLAN PUBLISHING

INDEX TO QUESTIONS AND ANSWERS

EXAM TECHNIQUE

- **Do not skip any of the material** in the syllabus.

- **Read each question** *very* carefully.

- **Double-check your answer** before committing yourself to it.

- Answer **every** question – if you do not know an answer to a multiple choice question or true/false question, you don't lose anything by guessing. Think carefully before you **guess**.

- If you are answering a multiple-choice question, **eliminate first those answers that you know are wrong**. Then choose the most appropriate answer from those that are left.

- **Don't panic** if you realise you've answered a question incorrectly. Getting one question wrong will not mean the difference between passing and failing.

Computer-based exams – tips

- Do not attempt a CBA until you have **completed all study material** relating to it.

- On the AAT website there is a CBA demonstration. It is **ESSENTIAL** that you attempt this before your real CBA. You will become familiar with how to move around the CBA screens and the way that questions are formatted, increasing your confidence and speed in the actual exam.

- Be sure you understand how to use the **software** before you start the exam. If in doubt, ask the assessment centre staff to explain it to you.

- Questions are **displayed on the screen** and answers are entered using keyboard and mouse. At the end of the exam, you are given a certificate showing the result you have achieved.

- In addition to the traditional multiple-choice question type, CBAs will also contain **other types of questions**, such as number entry questions, drag and drop, true/false, pick lists or drop down menus or hybrids of these.

- In some CBAs you will have to type in complete computations or written answers.

- You need to be sure you **know how to answer questions** of this type before you sit the exam, through practice.

KAPLAN'S RECOMMENDED REVISION APPROACH

QUESTION PRACTICE IS THE KEY TO SUCCESS

Success in professional examinations relies upon you acquiring a firm grasp of the required knowledge at the tuition phase. In order to be able to do the questions, knowledge is essential.

However, the difference between success and failure often hinges on your exam technique on the day and making the most of the revision phase of your studies.

The **Kaplan textbook** is the starting point, designed to provide the underpinning knowledge to tackle all questions. However, in the revision phase, poring over text books is not the answer.

Kaplan pocket notes are designed to help you quickly revise a topic area; however, you then need to practice questions. There is a need to progress to exam style questions as soon as possible and to tie your exam technique and technical knowledge together.

The importance of question practice cannot be over-emphasised.

The recommended approach below is designed by expert tutors in the field, in conjunction with their knowledge of the examiner and the specimen assessment.

You need to practise as many questions as possible in the time you have left.

OUR AIM

Our aim is to get you to the stage where you can attempt exam questions confidently, to time, in a closed book environment, with no supplementary help (i.e. to simulate the real examination experience).

Practising your exam technique is also vitally important for you to assess your progress and identify areas of weakness that may need more attention in the final run up to the examination.

In order to achieve this we recognise that initially you may feel the need to practice some questions with open book help.

Good exam technique is vital.

THE KAPLAN REVISION PLAN

Stage 1: Assess areas of strengths and weaknesses

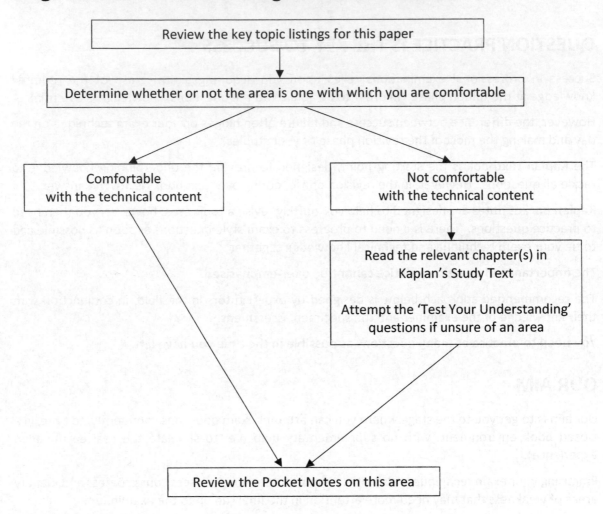

Stage 2: Practice questions

Follow the order of revision of topics as presented in this kit and attempt the questions in the order suggested.

Try to avoid referring to text books and notes and the model answer until you have completed your attempt.

Review your attempt with the model answer and assess how much of the answer you achieved.

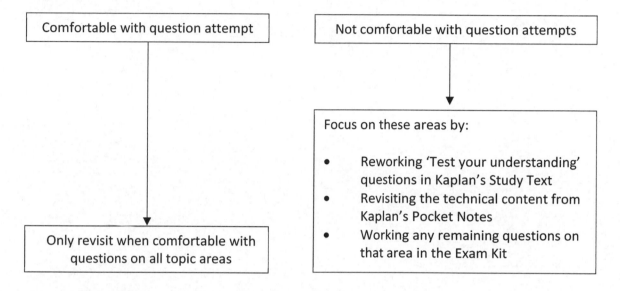

| Comfortable with question attempt | Not comfortable with question attempts |

Focus on these areas by:

- Reworking 'Test your understanding' questions in Kaplan's Study Text
- Revisiting the technical content from Kaplan's Pocket Notes
- Working any remaining questions on that area in the Exam Kit

Only revisit when comfortable with questions on all topic areas

Stage 3: Final pre-exam revision

We recommend that you **attempt at least one two hour 30 minute mock examination** containing a set of previously unseen exam standard questions.

Attempt the mock CBA online in timed, closed book conditions to simulate the real exam experience.

Section 1

CASE STUDY INFORMATION

This case study contains a scenario which is referred to within various questions within this exam kit.

Scenario

This information is based on the scenario of Healthyou Ltd (Healthyou).

Healthyou is a private limited company, based in Harrogate, which operates a small number of shops across the north of England selling health supplements. Its approach is to use only organic products approved for human consumption by the food standards regulator.

Company background

History

The business was started 15 years ago by Sam Shah and Pat Singh when they opened their first shop in Harrogate. Although the early years of the business were quite difficult, the trend towards individuals taking more responsibility for their health and wellbeing has boosted the popularity and use of health supplements. This has resulted in a dramatic rise in both sales and profits over the last four years.

This surge in popularity and significantly improved operational performance has led to a further ten shops opening across the north of England during the last three years. The shop locations are selected based upon age, income and employment demographics. The intention is to open another four shops in the next financial year.

From the beginning, Healthyou has always been focused on providing a wide range of health supplements to relieve a variety of ailments, particularly relating to exercise-related issues such as sore and tight muscles. This has proved to be an important part of the success of the business, with gym members and runners being a large proportion of its restaurant customers.

Recent developments

Last year, Healthyou decided to expand its product offering by allowing customers to order products online. The products can be purchased and ordered using 'click-and-collect' at a nominated store or, for a small additional charge, be delivered directly to the customer. Due to logistical issues with deliveries, the 'click-and-collect' service is currently only available from two of the shops. The online service has been a success, but has resulted in a 5% reduction in the number of customers purchasing products in shops since the online service was introduced.

The expansion of Healthyou into multiple shops has meant that additional staff have had to be recruited to manage this increased operational activity. Healthyou has also had to rent premises in Harrogate to act as the business's head office.

Resources

On 31 December 20X4, Healthyou had 78 employees.

Department	Number of staff
Purchasing	7
Storage and distribution	12
Retail	42
Marketing and development	6
Administration	11

Staff

Some of Healthyou's key personnel are listed below:

Managing Director	Sam Shah
Deputy Managing Director	Pat Singh
Finance Director	Yoshika Mane
Human Resources Director	Pat Smythe
Regional Operations Manager	Jun Khan
Commercial Manager	Clem Seddon
Financial Controller	Ping Alonso
Purchasing Manager	Kazu Kumar
Development Chef	Hiromi Patel
Accounts Payable Manager	Kyo Suarez
Accounts Payable Clerk	Bai Firminio
General Accounts Clerk	Setsuna Reina
Cashier	Daya Haaland
Payroll Manager	Zhong Salah

Sustainability

The business has always prided itself on being a good employer, supporting local suppliers and minimising its environmental impact. As the business grows, the challenge is to make sure those principles stay embedded within the business. This includes:

- minimal waste within its activities. All packaging such as cardboard, paper and plastic is recyclable.

- minimum hourly rate of £12.50 per hour for all staff, to be constantly reviewed and kept ahead of the national minimum living wage.

- offering customers the facility to bring their own containers to fill with e.g. cereals, reducing the need for packaging.

KAPLAN PUBLISHING

Section 2

PRACTICE QUESTIONS

ROLE AND RESPONSIBILITIES OF THE ACCOUNTING FUNCTION

THE ACCOUNTING FUNCTION

1   ETHICS

Which statement provides a definition of business ethics?

	✓
Business ethics is concerned with complying with the law in business situations.	
Business ethics is concerned with complying with the law and all relevant accounting regulations.	
Business ethics is concerned with making the most appropriate moral judgements in business situations.	
Business ethics is concerned with avoiding illegal transactions business situations.	

2   GOOD ETHICAL BEHAVIOUR

Which TWO statements are key features of good ethical behaviour?

	✓
Good ethical behaviour increases costs without any significant benefits to the organisation.	
Good ethical behaviour helps to enhance the reputation of the organisation	
Good ethical behaviour help to reduce the risk of problems arising in the organisation	
Good ethical behaviour may result in an organisation becoming uncompetitive.	

3 IMPORTANCE OF ETHICS

Why is good ethical behaviour within the accounting function important?

	✓
It ensures that the business will make a profit on its trading activities.	
It ensures that employees in the accounting function will not make errors when performing their work.	
It guarantees that the accounting records do not contain any errors omissions or misstatements.	
It helps to maintain the accuracy and reliability of the accounting records.	

4 SUSTAINABILITY

Which statement provides a definition of sustainability?

	✓
Sustainability is defined as minimising the financial cost of inputs to produce the required products and services.	
Sustainability is defined as meeting the needs of the present whilst minimising any adverse impact upon future generations to meet their own needs.	
Sustainability is defined as minimising waste and pollution when producing goods and services.	
Sustainability is defined as the business being able to continue in existence for as long as possible.	

5 GOOD SUSTAINABILITY PRACTICES

Which TWO of the following are good sustainability practices within the accounting function?

	✓
Having a paperless office, with employees using accounting software and email communication to do their work.	
Purchasing plastic office furniture as it is cheaper than wood and likely to last longer.	
Not installing double-glazing on the office windows.	
Using video conferencing for meetings, rather than employees meeting in person.	

6   IMPORTANCE OF SUSTAINABILITY

Which TWO statements identify why an organisation should have good sustainability policies and practices?

	✓
Good sustainable policies and practices will ensure that the organisation will make a profit on its trading activities.	
Good sustainability policies and practices will always result in choosing the lowest cost when purchasing materials and other business inputs.	
Good sustainability policies and practices help to improve the long-term viability of the organisation.	
Good sustainability policies and practices help to maintain and improve the reputation of the organisation.	

7   STAFF STRUCTURES I

Identify whether each of the following statements is true or false.

	True ✓	False ✓
A multinational organisation is likely to have a longer scalar chain than a single-site organisation.		
A 'flat' organisation will have a long scalar chain.		
A manager in a 'flat' organisation will always have a narrower span of control than a manager in a 'tall' organisation.		
A manager's span of control may include employees who work in different departments or in different locations.		

8   STAFF STRUCTURES II

Identify whether the following statements about a broad span of control are true or false

	True ✓	False ✓
It improves productivity for the organisation.		
It has fewer levels of management.		
It is less expensive to operate.		
Employees can easily give feedback on ways to improve systems.		

FINANCIAL INFORMATION USED BY STAKEHOLDERS

9   FINANCIAL INFORMATION I

Complete the following statements relating to financial information.

Monthly or quarterly accounts are normally prepared for the benefit of (GAP 1). These accounts help them to make decisions regarding (GAP2).

Picklist: GAP 1 business owners, potential investors, managers

Picklist: GAP 2 whether or not to invest in the business, controlling and managing the business

10   ACCOUNTS PRODUCED BY MANAGERS

State whether the following statements are true or false.

	True / False
The form and content of accounts produced by managers for decision-making and control purposes must comply with the law and with relevant accounting standards.	
Annual financial statements will contain exactly the same information as accounts produced by managers for decision-making and control purposes.	

11   FINANCIAL STATEMENTS I

Identify which financial statement can be used to enable a user to identify relevant financial information.

	Financial statement
The amount of cash paid to purchase property, plant and equipment during the year.	
The amount of trade payables at the year end	
By how much the cash balance has increased or decreased during the year.	
Whether or not land and buildings were revalued during the year.	

Picklist: Statement of profit or loss, Statement of financial position, Statement of cash flows, Statement of changes in equity

12 FINANCIAL STATEMENTS II

State which financial statement will be used to identify information for the calculation of the following accounting ratios.

	Financial statement
Gearing ratio	
Gross profit margin	
Current ratio	

13 CEEDEE LTD

Ceedee Ltd is a manufacturing company that uses a computer software package to record and process accounting transactions. The computer software package also produces periodic management accounts and annual financial accounts.

State whether or not each of the following situations would require Ceedee Ltd to change its existing accounting systems.

	Change systems / No change
The directors' decided to change the depreciation rate applicable to delivery vans.	
The recruitment of a new accounts clerk in the accounts department.	
The issue of an updated accounting standard dealing with the valuation of inventory.	

14 FINANCIAL INFORMATION II

State whether the following statements are true or false.

	True / False
Accounting information produced to assist decision-making by managers is likely to be more detailed than the annual financial statements.	
Annual financial statements contain all information that an external stakeholder would possibly need to make fully informed decisions.	

15 PERFORMANCE INDICATORS

Identify the relevant component required as part of the calculation for each of the following performance indicators

Current ratio	Gap 1
Inventory turnover	Gap 2
Trade receivables collection period	Gap 3
Return on capital employed	Gap 4

Gap 1	✓
Total current assets	
Cost of sales	
Operating profit	
Revenue	

Gap 2	✓
Total current assets	
Cost of sales	
Operating profit	
Revenue	

Gap 3	✓
Total current assets	
Cost of sales	
Operating profit	
Revenue	

Gap 4	✓
Total current assets	
Cost of sales	
Operating profit	
Revenue	

16 FINANCIAL INFORMATION III

Identify whether the following statements about financial information are correct.

	True / False
The budgetary control report will be presented to the Board of Directors.	
The Statement of Financial Position is used to determine the liquidity of an organisation.	

CHANGES TO MANAGEMENT INFORMATION

17   MANAGEMENT INFORMATION SYSTEMS I

State whether the following statements are true or false.

	True / False
It is not necessary for the management information system to distinguish between cash and credit sales when calculating the trade receivables collection period.	
If the management information system is able to classify liabilities as either current liabilities or non-current liabilities, this provides useful financial information for both internal and external stakeholders.	

18   MANAGEMENT INFORMATION SYSTEMS II

Complete the following statements relating to management information systems.

When an organisation changes its strategic objectives, it (GAP 1) require changes to its management information system. It is important that the management information system (GAP 2) change to meet the needs of internal stakeholders.

Picklist: GAP 1 will, will not

Picklist: GAP 2 does, does not

EVALUATE INTERNAL CONTROL SYSTEMS

INTERNAL CONTROLS

19 ORGANISATION SIZE

State whether the following statements are true or false.

	True / False
A small organisation does not need to have any internal controls.	
The accounting records in a large organisation which applies a range of effective internal controls in the accounting system will be guaranteed to be free from error.	
An online retailer can apply a range of effective internal controls within its accounting software systems.	

20 TYPES OF INTERNAL CONTROL

Match the type of internal control with the each of the control examples noted below.

	Type of control
An organisation operates a smartcard system with a barrier that prevents visitors accessing the building (other than reception area).	
As part of the selection and recruitment process, an organisation requires that applicants undergo an aptitude test and provide confirmation of their academic qualifications.	
Within the accounts department of an organisation, Huan is responsible for recording cash receipts from credit customers, Kiran is responsible for updating the sales ledger accounts and Nilam performs the monthly reconciliation of the sales ledger control account with the total of the sales ledger balances.	

Picklist: Authorisation and approval, Arithmetic and accounting, Supervision, Segregation of duties, Organisational, Physical, Personnel, Management

21 TYPES OF INTERNAL CONTROL

Match the type of internal control with the each of the control examples noted below.

	Type of control
An organisation requires that the purchase of any items of equipment which cost £500 or more is agreed in advance by a senior manager in advance of the purchase being made.	
When starting a new job, Guang was presented with a job description which specified individual responsibilities and identified the departmental manager to contact if there were any work-related problems.	
Within the accounting and finance department of an organisation, Akira oversees the work of a new member of staff and is able to offer practical guidance and instruction to ensure that transactions are processed correctly.	

Picklist: Authorisation and approval, Arithmetic and accounting, Supervision, Segregation of duties, Organisational, Physical, Personnel, Management

22 EFFECTIVE INTERNAL CONTROLS

State whether the following statements are true or false.

	True ✓	False ✓
If a large multi-site organisation has comprehensive authorisation and approval procedures for transactions, along with effective segregation of duties in the accounting and finance department, it will still need a range of other internal controls to help manage organisational activities effectively.		
An effective internal control system will prevent any fraud or error from occurring.		
In a small company with two directors and two employees in the accounting department it is still possible to have effective supervision and authorisation and approval controls in place.		

23 RESPONSIBILITY FOR THE INTERNAL CONTROL SYSTEM

Within a company, who is responsible for ensuring that it has an effective system of internal controls?

	✓
The external auditor	
The internal auditor	
The board of directors	
The finance director only	

24 INTERNAL CONTROLS 1

An internal control system in an organisation consists of five components: the control environment, the risk assessment process, the information system, control activities and monitoring of controls.

Match each of the following activities to the component that it illustrates.

	Control environment ✓	Information system ✓	Control activities ✓
Communication and enforcement of integrity and ethical values			
A requirement that all payments in excess of £1,000 require approval from two directors.			
The preparation of monthly management accounts			

25 INTERNAL CONTROLS 2

Healthyou is looking at introducing new internal controls to help reduce the risk of fraud.

Match each of the following activities to the type of control that it illustrates.

	Authorisation and approval ✓	Arithmetical and accounting ✓	Physical control ✓
The purchase ledger control clerk produces a reconciliation of the ledger account balances with the total on the payables ledger control account every month.			
The petty cash float is kept in a locked box within a safe when not required.			
The chief accountant extracts a trial balance from the ledger accounts before preparing the annual accounts.			

26   INTERNAL CONTROLS 3

Indicate whether the following limitations are true or false.

	True	False
If the costs of implementing a particular control exceed the benefits to be gained from its application, a business is unlikely to apply that control.		
The effectiveness of many controls do not rely upon the honesty and integrity of individuals applying them.		
Internal controls apply to all items, irrespective of their value.		
Standard controls are designed to deal with every possible transaction, no matter how unusual.		

27   INTERNAL CONTROLS 4

Sam Shah, Managing Director, is concerned that the business does not have a strong system of internal controls and has made suggestions for improvements to the current system. You have been asked to match the internal controls to the weakness that has been identified.

Identify which control is suitable for each of the following weaknesses.

Theft of inventory from an open warehouse.	Gap 1
Purchase orders are sent to suppliers without attaching a Purchase Order number.	Gap 2
Entry of a one-off transaction into the accounting system.	Gap 3
Supplier accounts are managed and paid by the same person.	Gap 4
Incorrect entry of sales invoices into sales daybook.	Gap 5
Non-compliance with appropriate accounting regulations and standards resulting from lack Of CPD.	Gap 6

Options	Gap No.
Management controls	
Segregation of duties	
Check arithmetical accuracy	
Physical access controls	
Authorisation and approval	
Competent personnel	

28 SMALL OR LARGE

As Healthyou has been expanding, you are reviewing its current internal controls and assessing their suitability as the company continues to develop and grow. Some new members of the management team have recently completed a management training course, where they were told that the type of internal controls needed depended on the size of the organisation in which they were used.

Identify whether the following internal controls are more suitable for a small or a large organisation.

Internal control	Small	Large
Monthly inventory checks		
Segregation of duties for the posting of purchase invoices, credit notes, preparing a supplier payment list and making payments to suppliers		
All purchase orders must be authorised by the Managing Director		

PREVENT AND DETECT FRAUD AND SYSTEMIC WEAKNESS

29 FRAUD 1

A clothes store in the city centre is trying to minimise the risk of clothes being stolen by shoppers.

Which TWO of the following would best reduce the risk of clothes being stolen from the store?

	✓
Segregation of duties between customer service staff on the shop floor and other members of staff taking payments from customers at tills.	
Requiring that all goods purchased are paid for by credit card or debit card, rather than cash.	
Each item of clothing has a security tag attached which can only be removed by a member of staff when the customer pays for the goods.	
In-store security guards and cameras monitor shoppers, particularly as they are leaving the store.	

30 FRAUD 2

The financial accountant of Onyx Ltd is concerned about the risk of fictitious overtime claims by employees.

Which TWO of the following control activities would best prevent this occurring?

	✓
The total cost of the payroll for the current month is compared with the total payroll cost for the previous month.	
All overtime claims must be reviewed and authorised by a manager prior to processing any payment.	
Review of working hours logged (e.g. by clock card, swipe card etc) by a responsible person.	
Supervision of the wages pay out by an independent official	

31 SYSTEMIC WEAKNESS

This task is about the types of fraud in the workplace together with ways to detect it.

Pat Singh, Healthyou's Deputy Managing Director, is concerned about the suitability of the internal controls and has identified the following weaknesses. You have been asked to explain why these weaknesses may have occurred.

Identify the cause of the following weaknesses:

Segregation of duties is deemed unnecessary.	Option 1
Management and supervision are remote.	Option 2
Staff create their own spreadsheets to prepare month-end reports instead of using Healthyou's accounting software.	Option 3
Inventory counts are rarely done.	Option 4

Option 1	✓
Lack of monitoring	
Lack of controls	
Lack of leadership	
Poor implementation of controls	

Option 2	✓
Lack of monitoring	
Lack of controls	
Lack of leadership	
Poor implementation of controls	

Option 3	✓
Lack of monitoring	
Lack of controls	
Lack of leadership	
Poor implementation of controls	

Option 4	✓
Lack of monitoring	
Lack of controls	
Lack of leadership	
Poor implementation of controls	

EVALUATE ACCOUNTING SYSTEMS AND PROCEDURES

EFFECTIVENESS OF THE ACCOUNTING SYSTEM

32   PURCHASE CYCLE CONTROLS 1

Healthyou has experienced occasions when payment was made for goods not received.

Which TWO of the following controls in a purchase cycle could be implemented to reduce the risk of payment of goods not received?

	✓
Sequentially pre-numbered purchase requisitions and sequence check.	
Matching of goods received note with purchase invoice.	
Goods are inspected for condition and quantity and agreed to purchase order before acceptance.	
Daily update of inventory system.	

33   PURCHASE CYCLE CONTROLS 2

Healthyou has experienced occasions when unnecessary goods and services were purchased.

Which TWO of the following controls in the purchase cycle could be implemented to reduce the risk of procurement of unnecessary goods and services?

	✓
Centralised purchasing department.	
Sequentially pre-numbered purchase requisitions and sequence check.	
Orders can only be placed with suppliers from the approved suppliers list.	
All purchase requisitions are signed as authorised by an appropriate manager.	

34 EXPENSE CLAIM CONTROLS

Kim Ono has been appointed as the new IT manager at Healthyou and really enjoys the job. The remuneration is not great, and other managers at the company have explained the way they 'get around' that issue. The sales manager explains to Kim that the key is to 'put everything on expenses – private petrol, drinks and even clothing. It's all fine and as long as you have a receipt, no-one in the finance department will question it' and continues by saying 'It's fine because the board are aware of it and turn a blind eye'.

Which ONE of the following essential internal control measures is evidently missing?

	✓
Healthyou lacks a control environment as the board are not setting an ethical tone at the top.	
Healthyou lacks an Internal Audit department.	
Healthyou lacks an experienced finance manager.	
Healthyou lacks an external auditor.	

35 HEALTHYOU – INVENTORY COUNTING PROCESSES

Each winter, Healthyou is obliged to count its inventory. This is typically done on the morning of 1 January.

For this business, inventory is held in a number of different places. Each location typically carries a range of products, including some goods received when customers have used the 'click-and-collect' service. Due to their nature, some products have a short 'use by' date and must be kept in chiller cabinet.

Each shop manager organises the inventory count at their own location using their permanent staff. In addition, this year, Healthyou arranged for an internal auditor to attend some of the inventory counts and feedback their findings. It was hoped that this would lead to improved procedures in the future. At one location, the local staff were short numbered and so the internal auditor acted as a counter and an auditor at the same time.

The count at each location was organised by having two teams. The first would count goods on the shop shelves and chiller cabinet, and the second in the back stores area.

For each location, sales information is detailed enough for head office to prepare pre-printed inventory sheets showing expected inventory levels for most products, so staff are expected to count these items and tick the relevant box if quantities match. Where there is a disagreement, the revised quantity should be added.

For the remaining products, such as fresh goods and health snacks, sales information does not allow head office to calculate exactly what quantities should be present. For these products a sheet of all possible products is generated and staff expected to complete the quantities.

Suppliers were requested not to deliver during the inventory counts. This policy was mostly followed but one supplier of did make a delivery to three locations during that day. The drivers offloaded the stock outside the store so as not to interfere with the counting process.

During the count, boxes of health drinks not yet unpacked were not opened but the slips on the side of the boxes were used to note the contents on the inventory sheets.

Goods were not individually checked for 'best by' or 'use by' dates but staff were asked to make a note of any items that looked 'past their best'.

Outline 3 weaknesses and their effect on the accounting systems in the boxes below:

Weakness	Effect of Weakness

36 BANK RECONCILIATION

Which ONE of the following statements explains the purpose of a bank reconciliation?

	✓
It is a control to ensure that the bank statement balance as at the end of the accounting year is correct.	
It is a control to ensure that all payments required have been made.	
It is a control to minimise the risk of errors and omissions in the cash book, and to identify such items for further investigation.	
It is a control to ensure that all unrecorded receipts are identified and recorded in the cash book.	

37 RECEIVABLES LEDGER CONTROL ACCOUNT RECONCILIATION

Which ONE of the following statements explains the purpose of the reconciliation of the trade receivables control account?

	✓
It is a control to ensure that receipts from credit customers have been accounted for.	
It is a control to ensure that invoices raised relating to credit customers have been accounted for.	
It is a control to ensure that entries in the control account agree with the total of the receivables' ledger, which guarantees that there are no errors or omissions in either the control account or the ledger account balances.	
It is a control to ensure that entries in the control account agree with the total of the receivables' ledger. Even if that's the case, the control account and/or ledger account balances may still contain errors or omissions.	

38 HERBUS SALES AND DESPATCH SYSTEM

The Board of Healthyou is considering buying a business that grows herbs and plants used for medicinal purposes. One potential target identified is Herbus, which sells its produce to a range of retail and other outlets, such as health clubs and to the end consumer. Herbus has a dedicated sales team to manage the relationship with larger customers but orders from smaller business customers and the public are mainly placed through Herbus' website, while some are also made via telephone.

Clem Seddon (Commercial Manager) has started to investigate the farm in more detail and has some concerns over its sales and despatch system. Clem is reasonably happy over the way sales to major customers are dealt with but has concerns over telephone and website transactions.

Online orders are automatically checked against inventory records and herb picking schedules for availability; telephone orders, however, are checked manually by order clerks after the call. A follow-up call is usually made to customers if there is insufficient inventory. When taking telephone orders, clerks note down the details on plain paper and afterwards they complete a three part pre-printed order form. These order forms are not sequentially numbered and are sent manually to both despatch and the accounts department.

As Herbus is expanding, customers are able to place online orders which will exceed their agreed credit limit by 10%. Online orders are automatically forwarded to the despatch and accounts department.

A daily pick list is printed by the despatch department and this is used by the warehouse team to despatch goods. The goods are accompanied by a despatch note and all customers are required to sign a copy of this. On return, the signed despatch notes are given to the warehouse team to file.

The sales quantities are entered from the despatch notes and the authorised sales prices are generated by the invoicing system. If a discount has been given, perhaps for a bulk order, then this has to be manually entered by the sales clerk onto the invoice.

Due to the expansion of the company, and as there is a large number of sale invoices, extra accounts staff have been asked to help out temporarily with producing the sales invoices. Normally it is only two sales clerks who produce the sales invoices.

Identify and explain FIVE deficiencies in Herbus' sales and despatch system and evaluate the impact of these deficiencies. (15 marks)

Deficiency	Evaluation of impact

39 PAYROLL FRAUD

You have recently discovered that the payroll clerk, Kim Mackie, has been overpaying herself by £400 each month. It has also been discovered that for nine months Kim has been paying someone named Scott Bennett an annual salary of £30,000, even though he is not an employee and has no payslips.

Identify which of the following procedures would detect the frauds identified above.

Procedures	Would detect ✓	Would not detect ✓
All payslips are checked by the Financial Controller for numerical accuracy.		
All payslips are sent using an online portal rather than being posted to employees' home addresses.		
The payment list is prepared by Kim and authorised by the Financial Controller before the payments are made.		
A check is performed to ensure that all employees are paid the minimum wage.		
A wages control account is completed.		
Payslips are prepared by Kim and checked against bank payments by the Financial Controller.		

40 HEALTHYOU'S GENERAL LEDGER SYSTEM

The general ledger of Healthyou is controlled by Healthyou general ledger is controlled by Yoshika Mane (Finance Director) and Ping Alonso (Financial Controller) with either of these people able to make independent journal entries. Yoshika and Ping are friends and keen snowboarders and skaters who like to get away over the winter period to snowboard and skate in various parts of the world. This isn't always easy to arrange as the year-end work needs to finish quickly to enable this holiday to take place. Pat Smythe (HR Director) is given access to the general ledger over this period in the unlikely event further adjustments are needed.

Yoshika does not require prior sight of the journals prepared by Ping as there is considerable trust between the two.

Anyone with general ledger access can create new general ledger accounts.

Non-current assets accounting policy

During the current year, the approach taken to accounting for non-current assets has been investigated by Yoshika. Having compared the approach taken by Healthyou to other similar businesses, Yoshika has decided to change a couple of matters:

- Firstly, smaller items of shop fittings and equipment would no longer be capitalised but, instead, written off as expenses.

- Secondly, the depreciation approach for larger items of equipment will be changed.

This decision was taken by Yishika just before the annual winter holiday and so instructed Pat to make the appropriate adjustments.

Identify and explain five weaknesses in the general ledger system and explain the impact of deficiency.

Weakness	Evaluation of impact

41 INVENTORY PURCHASES

Pat Singh, Healthyou's Deputy Managing Director, is concerned about the procedures that are in place in respect of inventory purchases, and has recently attended a fraud and money laundering event hosted by the auditors. Pat wants to ensure that the company does not become a victim of one of these offences, and has asked you to review the following procedures:

Purchases

Healthyou has a list of trusted suppliers that it deals with regularly.

When supplies are needed, orders are placed with these suppliers by staff over the telephone. No order number is required to place an order.

Goods received notes are filed together in date order but not matched with purchase invoices, as these are sent straight to the accounts department.

Invoices are entered onto the accounting system by Kyo Suarez, Accounts Payable Clerk. Before she pays the supplier, she checks the aged payables report against the supplier statements at the end of the month, to ensure that all invoices are on the system. The Finance Director is often busy, so Kyo has a payment limit that allows her authorise the bank payments below a certain amount.

If the warehouse team find any short deliveries, they notify the accounts team. The warehouse keep all the relevant paperwork so that they can monitor if certain suppliers regularly make short deliveries. In order to save the warehouse staff time, the accounts team will request a credit note for both these and any damaged goods. There are a number of ongoing disputes with suppliers about missing items and damaged goods.

If a part is needed urgently in order to allow production to continue, one of the warehouse staff takes money from petty cash and collects the part from a local supplier to avoid disrupting production. All staff have access to the petty cash tin as this is a frequent occurrence and it is vital that a lengthy petty cash process does not delay the process. Petty cash always reconciles with an acceptable difference, although staff often have to be chased for receipts.

(i) **Identify TWO types of fraud that may occur in the above situation.** (2 marks)

(ii) **Describe TWO circumstances that may allow each type of fraud identified to occur.**

Type of fraud	Circumstances

42   INVENTORY PURCHASES

You have recently discovered that Happy Oats, one of your suppliers, is the family business of Kazu Kumar, Healthyou's Purchasing Manager.

Kazu has been placing most bulk oat orders with Happy Oats because they offer a fast delivery service. Sometimes deliveries are made to Kazu's home address as goods can be received more quickly. Kazu also thinks that they will be offering the best price for the oats because of the family connection.

Healthyou purchase bulk oats from Happy Oats, but because the oats are sold at low prices Happy Oats have a policy that only goods damaged on delivery can be returned. Currently Healthyou do not have the facilities to accurately measure waste.

Happy Oats advertise themselves as the cheapest oat supplier in the area, and in order to keep costs down, they source all their oats from overseas suppliers who are not restricted by minimum wage regulations.

(i)   Identify THREE potential risks in the system outlined above.

(ii)   Identify the potential implication of each risk identified.

(iii)   Recommend an appropriate safeguard to minimise each risk.

Potential risk	Potential implication	Safeguard to minimise risk

43   NON-CURRENT ASSETS

This task is about the monitoring of accounting systems and how they work in practice.

Pat Singh, Deputy Managing Director, has raised a concern about the accuracy of the value of non-current assets shown in the financial statements. You have been asked to review the way in which non-current assets are recorded on acquisition and the system in place to identify disposals.

Purchase and recording of assets

Non-current assets with a value of £100,000 or above must be authorised by Yoshika Mane (Finance Director). All other assets are authorised by the departmental manager. For example, Jun Khan, Regional Operations Manager, would authorise the purchase of new delivery vans.

The delivery of new assets is arranged for a time when the departmental manager is available to check them. This ensures that all new assets are undamaged on receipt. At this stage, the departmental manager matches the Purchase Order to the Goods Received Note before filing them for future reference.

Invoices received on delivery are passed to Bai Firminio, Accounts Payable Clerk, to process and pay in accordance with the supplier's policies. Bai ensures that the invoices are entered into the accounting software. As the invoice has come from the departmental manager Bai is confident that the invoice simply needs coding for entry into the accounting software.

The item is also recorded on the non-current asset register by Ping Alonso, Financial Controller, who decides the appropriate method and rate of depreciation for the new asset.

Ping also checks that all assets are still in use each year. This check is completed around the same time as the year-end inventory count. After all non-current assets have been confirmed as still in use, Ping then calculates the deprecation based on the rate decided when the asset was initially purchased.

Disposal of assets

When an asset is sold, a sales invoice is raised and recorded by Setsuna Reina, General Accounts Clerk.

Ping Alonso then removes the asset from the non-current asset register, calculates the profit or loss on disposal, then prepares the journal to remove the asset from the financial statements.

(i)   Identify THREE weaknesses in the system for the accurate recording of non-current assets outlined above.

(ii)   Evaluate the impact that each of the weaknesses described in part (i) could have on the organisation.

UNDERSTAND THE IMPACT OF TECHNOLOGY ON ACCOUNTING SYSTEMS

44 NON-FINANCE PROFESSIONALS

Complete the following statements by selecting the correct option for each of the gaps below.

The best way to present financial data to non-finance professionals within your organisation is through a <<GAP 1 >>. You should consider the user's needs: determine what they need to see and then aim to <<GAP 2>>.

In order to check that the information you are presenting is in a suitable format for users to understand and interpret during the presentation, it is useful to <<GAP 3>>. You should then ensure that someone with limited technical knowledge can give you <<GAP 4>>.

Gap 1	✓
data dashboard	
pivot table	

Gap 2	✓
add interactive graphics	
eliminate clutter and distraction	

Gap 3	✓
check that you have given a definition for all the technical terms	
show it to someone who hasn't seen it before	

Gap 4	✓
a summary of the information contained within the presentation	
definitions for all the technical terms included in the presentation	

45 PASSWORDS

You have been asked to set up a new system of passwords for Healthyou's accounting system.

Which TWO of the following would reduce the effectiveness of passwords?

	✓
Requirement that passwords are changed every two weeks	
Users are allowed to choose their own passwords	
Automatic lock-out after 3 failed attempts to access system	
Making the sharing of passwords a disciplinary offence	
Displaying the password on the screen when entered	

46 MACHINE LEARNING

Identify whether the following statements about machine learning are true or false.

	True	False
Machine learning is a useful audit tool.		
Machine learning cannot support multi-dimensional or multi-variety data.		
The use of machine learning to code raw data will improve the accuracy of the reports produced.		
Machine learning does not enable continuous improvement.		
Humans do not need to be involved in decisions made using machine learning.		
Machine learning predictive models can be used to forecast revenue.		

47 DATA ANALYTICS

Identify the relevant component required as part of the calculation for each of the following performance indicators

The reliance on algorithmic predictions when using data analytics to analyse a wide selection of data is a cause for...	Gap 1	...particularly if the outcome is then considered...	Gap 2

Gap 1	✓
accuracy concerns,	
ethical concerns,	

Gap 2	✓
biased and unfair.	
inaccurate and may be misleading.	

48 INFORMATION

The provision of information in a more appealing and understandable manner is often referred to as what?

	✓
Artificial Intelligence	
Cloud computing	
Data visualisation	
Data simplification	

49 INFORMATION

Raj has been analysing trends in the online reviews on social media for Healthyou's main product line. However, he has noticed many inconsistencies.

Which of the 4 Vs of big data may be causing this problem?

	✓
Volume	
Variety	
Velocity	
Veracity	

50 WORKING FROM HOME

Increasing numbers of Healthyou's staff are considering working from home, so you are reviewing the policy for data and asset security.

Identify which of the following are required for the security of finance data stored on your company laptop when working from home.

Statement	Required ✓	Not required ✓
Lock your screen if leaving your laptop unattended.		
Ensure data is stored on an encrypted hard drive.		
Ensure access to USB ports has been restricted.		

51 DATA VISUALISATION

Which of the following is a benefit of data visualisation for the finance function?

	✓
Weekly or monthly reporting will be produced on time	
Improved data security	
Improved fraud detection	
Improved insight and understanding	

52   CLOUD COMPUTING

Which of the following is a disadvantage of cloud computing?

	✓
Increased flexibility to working arrangements	
More reliance on third party suppliers	
Access to continually up to date software	
Easier integration of systems	

RECOMMEND IMPROVEMENTS TO ACCOUNTING SYSTEMS

CHANGES TO THE ACCOUNTING SYSTEM

53 SWOT ANALYSIS

What is a SWOT analysis?

	✓
It is a management method whereby an organization can assess major external factors that influence its operation in order to become more competitive in the market.	
It is an analysis framework that matches an organisation's goals, programmes and capacities to the environment in which it operates.	
It is a framework or tool used to analyse and monitor the macro-environmental factors that may have a profound impact on an organisation's performance.	

54 PESTLE ANALYSIS

What is a PESTLE analysis?

	✓
It is a management method whereby an organization can assess major external factors that influence its operation in order to become more competitive in the market.	
It is an analysis framework that matches an organisation's goals, programmes and capacities to the environment in which it operates.	
It is a framework or tool used to analyse and monitor the macro-environmental factors that may have a profound impact on an organisation's performance.	

55 PEST ANALYSIS

What is a PEST analysis?

	✓
It is a management method whereby an organization can assess major external factors that influence its operation in order to become more competitive in the market.	
It is an analysis framework that matches an organisation's goals, programmes and capacities to the environment in which it operates.	
It is a framework or tool used to analyse and monitor the macro-environmental factors that may have a profound impact on an organisation's performance.	

THE EFFECTS OF CHANGES ON USERS OF THE SYSTEM

56 CHANGEOVER

The directors of Healthyou are considering updating the accounting system.

Yoshika Mane (FD) is suggesting that the direct changeover method be adopted. However, Sam Shah (Managing Director) has argued that direct changeover is usually the highest risk alternative available.

Which TWO of the following controls can mitigate the risk of system failure during direct changeover?

	✓
Training	
Testing	
Check digits	
System documentation	
Data backup	

57 INFORMATION SYSTEM CONTROLS

Management information system controls may be classified as 'security controls' and 'integrity controls'.

Identify the correct category for the following controls.

	Security ✓	Integrity ✓
Locked doors		
Fire alarms		
Passwords		
Authorisation of data entry		
Batch totals		
Check digits		
Reconciliation		
CCTV		

58 SALES ORDER PROCESSING

This task Is about the analysis of internal controls with recommendations to improve whilst considering the impact on users.

You have been asked to carry out a review of Healthyou's sales order processing and make recommendations for improvement.

Your findings are below.

Background data

Currently, as well as retail sales through shops, sales are made to commercial customers across the world. Although the overseas market is expanding, Healthyou would like to develop its online market following recent development of an online platform.

As the business is also looking to improve its sustainability, it feels that an increased online presence will support this alongside other measures, such as the implementation of LED and sensor lighting, upgraded building insulation, and the introduction of recycled packaging.

Sales and orders

Catalogues will all be produced electronically and are available on the website or can be sent to customers by email. The website has a comprehensive list of products and is up to date with items that are out of stock. The website also gives dates when the items are expected back into stock and estimated delivery times.

Orders can now be placed via the website or email. No other order methods are accepted.

New customers and new products

All new customers are given a credit limit of £500 and 14 days to pay while initial credit checks are completed.

Credit checks are completed by an agency and a suggested credit limit is given. Once a month, the credit limits are updated on the system by Kate Santiago, Credit Controller. When this is done, she emails any customers who are over their credit limit to ask for an immediate payment.

As the market is increasingly competitive, a number of new bespoke products are being considered as this will potentially give access to a new market with few competitors.

Complete a SWOT analysis for the procedures outlined above.

(i)   Identify ONE strength, ONE weakness, ONE opportunity to improve the procedures, and ONE threat to the effectiveness in the procedures outlined above.

(ii)   Explain how the strength benefits the organisation.

(iii)   Describe the potential damage this weakness could cause the organisation and a potential remedy.

(iv)   For the opportunity, explain how the procedure should be changed and how this would benefit the organisation

(v)   Explain how the threat could damage the organisation and an action that could reduce the risk.

(i) Strength	(ii) Benefit
(i) Weakness	(iii) Damage and remedy
(i) Opportunity	(iv) Change and benefit
(i) Threat	(v) Damage and action

59 COST-BENEFIT ANALYSIS

A Cost Benefit Analysis (CBA) has also been produced to support other decisions that are being made on the continued expansion of Healthyou. Sam Shah (Managing Director) has heard the issues identified can be categorised into Social, Environmental and Corporate, or People, Planet, Profit. You have been asked to categorise these findings.

The following statements are the results of the Cost Benefit Analysis.

Identify the appropriate category for each of the following statements.

Statement	Social ✔	Environmental ✔	Corporate ✔
Ability to recycle waste materials.			
Reduced inventory levels resulting in reduced storage costs.			
Automation of production resulting in redundancies.			
Change of delivery method to use electric vehicles.			
Improved efficiencies following training staff resulting in cost savings.			

60 PESTLE

Sam Shah (Managing Director of Healthyou) is not familiar with PESTLE and has asked you to show which category is appropriate for the statements given below.

Identify the appropriate category for each statement from the PESTLE analysis findings.

Statement	Political ✔	Economical ✔	Social ✔	Technological ✔	Legal ✔	Environmental ✔
Initiative to reduce carbon footprint.						
Trade uncertainties in SMEs as result of changing legislation.						
Changes due to Government legislation such as digital tax reporting.						
Increased automation resulting in redundant admin tasks.						
Investment in low energy products.						

Section 3

ANSWERS TO PRACTICE QUESTIONS

ROLE AND RESPONSIBILITIES OF THE ACCOUNTING FUNCTION

THE ACCOUNTING FUNCTION

1 ETHICS

Which statement provides a definition of business ethics?

	✓
Business ethics is concerned with complying with the law in business situations.	
Business ethics is concerned with complying with the law and all relevant accounting regulations.	
Business ethics is concerned with making the most appropriate moral judgements in business situations.	✓
Business ethics is concerned with avoiding illegal transactions business situations.	

2 GOOD ETHICAL BEHAVIOUR

Which TWO statements are key features of good ethical behaviour?

	✓
Good ethical behaviour increases costs without any significant benefits to the organisation.	
Good ethical behaviour helps to enhance the reputation of the organisation	✓
Good ethical behaviour help to reduce the risk of problems arising in the organisation	✓
Good ethical behaviour may result in an organisation becoming uncompetitive.	

3   IMPORTANCE OF ETHICS

Why is good ethical behaviour within the accounting function important?

	✓
It ensures that the business will make a profit on its trading activities.	
It ensures that employees in the accounting function will not make errors when performing their work.	
It guarantees that the accounting records do not contain any errors omissions or misstatements.	
It helps to maintain the accuracy and reliability of the accounting records.	✓

4   SUSTAINABILITY

Which statement provides a definition of sustainability?

	✓
Sustainability is defined as minimising the financial cost of inputs to produce the required products and services.	
Sustainability is defined as meeting the needs of the present whilst minimising any adverse impact upon future generations to meet their own needs.	✓
Sustainability is defined as minimising waste and pollution when producing goods and services.	
Sustainability is defined as the business being able to continue in existence for as long as possible.	

5   GOOD SUSTAINABILITY PRACTICES

Which TWO of the following are good sustainability practices within the accounting function?

	✓
Having a paperless office, with employees using accounting software and email communication to do their work.	✓
Purchasing plastic office furniture as it is cheaper than wood and likely to last longer.	
Not installing double-glazing on the office windows.	
Using video conferencing for meetings, rather than employees meeting in person.	✓

6   IMPORTANCE OF SUSTAINABILITY

Which TWO statements identify why an organisation should have good sustainability policies and practices?

	✓
Good sustainable policies and practices will ensure that the organisation will make a profit on its trading activities.	
Good sustainability policies and practices will always result in choosing the lowest cost when purchasing materials and other business inputs.	
Good sustainability policies and practices help to improve the long-term viability of the organisation.	✓
Good sustainability policies and practices help to maintain and improve the reputation of the organisation.	✓

7   STAFF STRUCTURES I

Identify whether each of the following statements is true or false.

	True ✓	False ✓
A multinational organisation is likely to have a longer scalar chain than a single-site organisation.	✓	
A 'flat' organisation will have a long scalar chain.		✓
A manager in a 'flat' organisation will always have a narrower span of control than a manager in a 'tall' organisation.		✓
A manager's span of control may include employees who work in different departments or in different locations.	✓	

8   STAFF STRUCTURES II

Identify whether the following statements about a broad span of control are true or false

	True ✓	False ✓
It improves productivity for the organisation.		✓
It has fewer levels of management.	✓	
It is less expensive to operate.	✓	
Employees can easily give feedback on ways to improve systems.		✓

FINANCIAL INFORMATION USED BY STAKEHOLDERS

9   FINANCIAL INFORMATION I

Complete the following statements relating to financial information.

Monthly or quarterly accounts are normally prepared for the benefit of (GAP 1). These accounts help them to make decisions regarding (GAP2).

Picklist: GAP 1 business owners, potential investors, managers

Picklist: GAP 2 whether or not to invest in the business, controlling and managing the business

10   ACCOUNTS PRODUCED BY MANAGERS

State whether the following statements are true or false.

	True / False
The form and content of accounts produced by managers for decision-making and control purposes must comply with the law and with relevant accounting standards.	False
Annual financial statements will contain exactly the same information as accounts produced by managers for decision-making and control purposes.	False

11   FINANCIAL STATEMENTS I

Identify which financial statement can be used to enable a user to identify relevant financial information.

	Financial statement
The amount of cash paid to purchase property, plant and equipment during the year.	Statement of cash flows
The amount of trade payables at the year end	Statement of financial position
By how much the cash balance has increased or decreased during the year.	Statement of cash flows
Whether or not land and buildings were revalued during the year.	Statement of changes in equity

Picklist: Statement of profit or loss, Statement of financial position, Statement of cash flows, Statement of changes in equity

12 FINANCIAL STATEMENTS II

State which financial statement will be used to identify information for the calculation of the following accounting ratios.

	Financial statement
Gearing ratio	Statement of financial position
Gross profit margin	Statement of profit or loss
Current ratio	Statement of financial position

13 CEEDEE LTD

State whether or not each of the following situations would require Ceedee Ltd to change its existing accounting systems.

	Change systems / No change
The directors' decided to change the depreciation rate applicable to delivery vans.	Change systems
The recruitment of a new accounts clerk in the accounts department.	No change
The issue of an updated accounting standard dealing with the valuation of inventory.	Change systems

14 FINANCIAL INFORMATION II

State whether the following statements are true or false.

	True / False
Accounting information produced to assist decision-making by managers is likely to be more detailed than the annual financial statements.	True
Annual financial statements contain all information that an external stakeholder would possibly need to make fully informed decisions.	False

15 PERFORMANCE INDICATORS

Identify the relevant component required as part of the calculation for each of the following performance indicators

Current ratio	Gap 1
Inventory turnover	Gap 2
Trade receivables collection period	Gap 3
Return on capital employed	Gap 4

Gap 1	✓
Total current assets	✓
Cost of sales	
Operating profit	
Revenue	

Gap 2	✓
Total current assets	
Cost of sales	✓
Operating profit	
Revenue	

Gap 3	✓
Total current assets	
Cost of sales	
Operating profit	
Revenue	✓

Gap 4	✓
Total current assets	
Cost of sales	
Operating profit	✓
Revenue	

16 FINANCIAL INFORMATION III

Identify whether the following statements about financial information are correct.

	True / False
The budgetary control report will be presented to the Board of Directors.	True
The Statement of Financial Position is used to determine the liquidity of an organisation.	True

CHANGES TO MANAGEMENT INFORMATION

17   MANAGEMENT INFORMATION SYSTEMS I

State whether the following statements are true or false.

	True / False
It is not necessary for the management information system to distinguish between cash and credit sales when calculating the trade receivables collection period.	False
If the management information system is able to classify liabilities as either current liabilities or non-current liabilities, this provides useful financial information for both internal and external stakeholders.	True

18   MANAGEMENT INFORMATION SYSTEMS II

Complete the following statements relating to management information systems.

When an organisation changes its strategic objectives, it (GAP 1) require changes to its management information system. It is important that the management information system (GAP 2) change to meet the needs of internal stakeholders.

Picklist: GAP 1 will, will not

Picklist: GAP 2 does, does not

EVALUATE INTERNAL CONTROL SYSTEMS

INTERNAL CONTROLS

19   ORGANISATION SIZE

State whether the following statements are true or false.

	True / False
A small organisation does not need to have any internal controls.	False
The accounting records in a large organisation which applies a range of effective internal controls in the accounting system will be guaranteed to be free from error.	False
An online retailer can apply a range of effective internal controls within its accounting software systems.	True

20   TYPES OF INTERNAL CONTROL

Match the type of internal control with the each of the control examples noted below.

	Type of control
An organisation operates a smartcard system with a barrier that prevents visitors accessing the building (other than reception area).	Physical
As part of the selection and recruitment process, an organisation requires that applicants undergo an aptitude test and provide confirmation of their academic qualifications.	Personnel
Within the accounts department of an organisation, Huan is responsible for recording cash receipts from credit customers, Kiran is responsible for updating the sales ledger accounts and Nilam performs the monthly reconciliation of the sales ledger control account with the total of the sales ledger balances.	Segregation of duties

Picklist: Authorisation and approval, Arithmetic and accounting, Supervision, Segregation of duties, Organisational, Physical, Personnel, Management

21 TYPES OF INTERNAL CONTROL

Match the type of internal control with the each of the control examples noted below.

	Type of control
An organisation requires that the purchase of any items of equipment which cost £500 or more is agreed in advance by a senior manager in advance of the purchase being made.	Authorisation and approval
When starting a new job, Guang was presented with a job description which specified individual responsibilities and identified the departmental manager to contact if there were any work-related problems.	Organisational
Within the accounting and finance department of an organisation, Akira oversees the work of a new member of staff and is able to offer practical guidance and instruction to ensure that transactions are processed correctly.	Supervision

Picklist: Authorisation and approval, Arithmetic and accounting, Supervision, Segregation of duties, Organisational, Physical, Personnel, Management

22 EFFECTIVE INTERNAL CONTROLS

State whether the following statements are true or false.

	True ✓	False ✓
If a large multi-site organisation has comprehensive authorisation and approval procedures for transactions, along with effective segregation of duties in the accounting and finance department, it will still need a range of other internal controls to help manage organisational activities effectively.	✓	
An effective internal control system will prevent any fraud or error from occurring.		✓
In a small company with two directors and two employees in the accounting department it is still possible to have effective supervision and authorisation and approval controls in place.	✓	

23 RESPONSIBILITY FOR THE INTERNAL CONTROL SYSTEM

Within a company, who is responsible for ensuring that it has an effective system of internal controls?

	✓
The external auditor	
The internal auditor	
The board of directors	✓
The finance director only	

24 INTERNAL CONTROLS 1

Match each of the following activities to the component that it illustrates.

	Control environment ✓	Information system ✓	Control activities ✓
Communication and enforcement of integrity and ethical values	✓		
A requirement that all payments in excess of £1,000 require approval from two directors.			✓
The preparation of monthly management accounts		✓	

25 INTERNAL CONTROLS 2

Match each of the following activities to the type of control that it illustrates.

	Authorisation and approval ✓	Arithmetical and accounting ✓	Physical control ✓
The purchase ledger control clerk produces a reconciliation of the ledger account balances with the total on the payables ledger control account every month.		✓	
The petty cash float is kept in a locked box within a safe when not required.			✓
The chief accountant extracts a trial balance from the ledger accounts before preparing the annual accounts.		✓	

26 INTERNAL CONTROLS 3

Indicate whether the following limitations are true or false.

	True	False
If the costs of implementing a particular control exceed the benefits to be gained from its application, a business is unlikely to apply that control.	✓	
The effectiveness of many controls do not rely upon the honesty and integrity of individuals applying them.		✓
Internal controls apply to all items, irrespective of their value.	✓	
Standard controls are designed to deal with every possible transaction, no matter how unusual.		✓

27 INTERNAL CONTROLS 4

Identify which control is suitable for each of the following weaknesses.

Theft of inventory from an open warehouse.	Gap 1
Purchase orders are sent to suppliers without attaching a Purchase Order number.	Gap 2
Entry of a one-off transaction into the accounting system.	Gap 3
Supplier accounts are managed and paid by the same person.	Gap 4
Incorrect entry of sales invoices into sales daybook.	Gap 5
Non-compliance with appropriate accounting regulations and standards resulting from lack Of CPD.	Gap 6

Options	Gap No.
Management controls	Gap 3
Segregation of duties	Gap 4
Check arithmetical accuracy	Gap 5
Physical access controls	Gap 1
Authorisation and approval	Gap 2
Competent personnel	Gap 6

28   SMALL OR LARGE

Identify whether the following internal controls are more suitable for a small or a large organisation.

Internal control	Small	Large
Monthly inventory checks		✓
Segregation of duties for the posting of purchase invoices, credit notes, preparing a supplier payment list and making payments to suppliers		✓
All purchase orders must be authorised by the Managing Director	✓	

PREVENT AND DETECT FRAUD AND SYSTEMIC WEAKNESS

29   FRAUD 1

Which TWO of the following would best reduce the risk of clothes being stolen from the store?

	✓
Segregation of duties between customer service staff on the shop floor and other members of staff taking payments from customers at tills.	
Requiring that all goods purchased are paid for by credit card or debit card, rather than cash.	
Each item of clothing has a security tag attached which can only be removed by a member of staff when the customer pays for the goods.	✓
In-store security guards and cameras monitor shoppers, particularly as they are leaving the store.	✓

30   FRAUD 2

Which TWO of the following control activities would best prevent this occurring?

	✓
The total cost of the payroll for the current month is compared with the total payroll cost for the previous month.	
All overtime claims must be reviewed and authorised by a manager prior to processing any payment.	✓
Review of working hours logged (e.g. by clock card, swipe card etc) by a responsible person.	✓
Supervision of the wages pay out by an independent official	

31 SYSTEMIC WEAKNESS

Identify the cause of the following weaknesses:

Segregation of duties is deemed unnecessary.	Option 1
Management and supervision are remote.	Option 2
Staff create their own spreadsheets to prepare month-end reports instead of using Healthyou's accounting software.	Option 3
Inventory counts are rarely done.	Option 4

Option 1	✓
Lack of monitoring	
Lack of controls	✓
Lack of leadership	
Poor implementation of controls	

Option 2	✓
Lack of monitoring	
Lack of controls	
Lack of leadership	✓
Poor implementation of controls	

Option 3	✓
Lack of monitoring	
Lack of controls	
Lack of leadership	
Poor implementation of controls	✓

Option 4	✓
Lack of monitoring	✓
Lack of controls	
Lack of leadership	
Poor implementation of controls	

EVALUATE ACCOUNTING SYSTEMS AND PROCEDURES

EFFECTIVENESS OF THE ACCOUNTING SYSTEM

32 PURCHASE CYCLE CONTROLS 1

Which TWO of the following controls in a purchase cycle could be implemented to reduce the risk of payment of goods not received?

	✓
Sequentially pre-numbered purchase requisitions and sequence check.	
Matching of goods received note with purchase invoice.	✓
Goods are inspected for condition and quantity and agreed to purchase order before acceptance.	✓
Daily update of inventory system.	

33 PURCHASE CYCLE CONTROLS 2

Healthyou has experienced occasions when unnecessary goods and services were purchased.

Which TWO of the following controls in the purchase cycle could be implemented to reduce the risk of procurement of unnecessary goods and services?

	✓
Centralised purchasing department.	
Sequentially pre-numbered purchase requisitions and sequence check.	
Orders can only be placed with suppliers from the approved suppliers list.	
All purchase requisitions are signed as authorised by an appropriate manager.	✓

34 EXPENSE CLAIM CONTROLS

Kim Ono has been appointed as the new IT manager at Healthyou and really enjoys the job. The remuneration is not great, and other managers at the company have explained the way they 'get around' that issue. The sales manager explains to Kim that the key is to 'put everything on expenses – private petrol, drinks and even clothing. It's all fine and as long as you have a receipt, no-one in the finance department will question it' and continues by saying 'It's fine because the board are aware of it and turn a blind eye'.

Which ONE of the following essential internal control measures is evidently missing?

	✓
Healthyou lacks a control environment as the board are not setting an ethical tone at the top.	✓
Healthyou lacks an Internal Audit department.	
Healthyou lacks an experienced finance manager.	
Healthyou lacks an external auditor.	

35 HEALTHYOU – INVENTORY COUNTING PROCESSES

Outline 3 weaknesses and their effect on the accounting systems in the boxes below:

Weakness	Effect of Weakness
The shop manager and staff should not be involved in the count at their own location.	It would be very easy for a member of staff to cover up a fraud – for example, had they stolen anything, then it would be easy to tick the pre-prepared inventory count sheet indicating the item was still on the premises. This would lead to an over-valuation of inventory.
The internal auditor should attend as an observer only and not get involved in the count itself. To do so confuses the roles of the people involved.	Errors in process might not have been detected as the internal auditor was busy "doing" rather than "observing". It is also possible that the internal auditor who is not an employee is not competent to recognise damaged or slow moving inventory and so these items could go unrecorded.
The instructions are capable of being misinterpreted. When viewing loose 'help yourself' items where customers can bring their own containers, it would be very difficult for staff to estimate the quantity.	Staff may not estimate qualities of 'loose' products, unless they have appropriate experience or trading. This could lead to misstatement of the inventory values.

36 BANK RECONCILIATION

Which ONE of the following statements explains the purpose of a bank reconciliation?

	✓
It is a control to ensure that the bank statement balance as at the end of the accounting year is correct.	
It is a control to ensure that all payments required have been made.	
It is a control to minimise the risk of errors and omissions in the cash book, and to identify such items for further investigation.	✓
It is a control to ensure that all unrecorded receipts are identified and recorded in the cash book.	

37 RECEIVABLES LEDGER CONTROL ACCOUNT RECONCILIATION

Which ONE of the following statements explains the purpose of the reconciliation of the trade receivables control account?

	✓
It is a control to ensure that receipts from credit customers have been accounted for.	
It is a control to ensure that invoices raised relating to credit customers have been accounted for.	
It is a control to ensure that entries in the control account agree with the total of the receivables' ledger, which guarantees that there are no errors or omissions in either the control account or the ledger account balances.	
It is a control to ensure that entries in the control account agree with the total of the receivables' ledger. Even if that's the case, the control account and/or ledger account balances may still contain errors or omissions.	✓

38 HERBUS SALES AND DESPATCH SYSTEM

Identify and explain FIVE deficiencies in Herbus' sales and despatch system and evaluate the impact of these deficiencies. **(15 marks)**

Deficiency	Evaluation of impact
Inventory availability for telephone orders is not checked at the time the order is placed. The order clerks manually check the availability later and only then inform customers if there is insufficient inventory available.	There is the risk that where goods are not available, order clerks could forget to contact the customers, leading to unfulfilled orders. This could lead to customer dissatisfaction, and would impact the farm's reputation.
Telephone orders are not recorded immediately on the three part pre-printed order forms; these are completed after the telephone call.	There is a risk that incorrect or insufficient details may be recorded by the clerk and this could result in incorrect orders being despatched or orders failing to be despatched at all, resulting in a loss of customer goodwill.
Telephone orders are not sequentially numbered.	Therefore if orders are misplaced whilst in transit to the despatch department, these orders will not be fulfilled, resulting in dissatisfied customers.
Customers are able to place online orders which will exceed their agreed credit limit by 10%.	This increases the risk of accepting orders from bad credit risks. If they default on payment, there will be a write-off of irrecoverable debts.
A daily pick list is used by the despatch department when sending out customer orders. However, it does not appear that the goods are checked back to the original order.	This increases the risk that incorrect goods are sent to customers, leading to customer dissatisfaction.

Additional staff have been drafted in to help the two sales clerks produce the sales invoices.	As the extra staff will not be as experienced as the sales clerks, there is an increased risk of mistakes being made when invoices are raised with customers being under or over-charged.
Discounts given to customers are manually entered onto the sales invoices by sales clerks. In addition, a clerk could forget to manually enter the discount or enter an incorrect level of discount for a customer.	This could result in unauthorised sales discounts being given as there does not seem to be any authorisation required. If the discount is not entered manually by the sales clerk, the sales invoice will be overstated and a loss of customer goodwill.

39 PAYROLL FRAUD

Identify which of the following procedures would detect the frauds identified above.

Procedures	Would detect ✓	Would not detect ✓
All payslips are checked by the Financial Controller for numerical accuracy.		✓
All payslips are sent using an online portal rather than being posted to employees' home addresses.		✓
The payment list is prepared by Kim and authorised by the Financial Controller before the payments are made.	✓	
A check is performed to ensure that all employees are paid the minimum wage.		✓
A wages control account is completed.	✓	
Payslips are prepared by Kim and checked against bank payments by the Financial Controller.	✓	

40   HEALTHYOU'S GENERAL LEDGER SYSTEM

Identify and explain five weaknesses in the general ledger system and explain the impact of deficiency.

Weakness	Evaluation of impact
There appears to be no approval required for any journal entries made by Yoshika (or for that matter Pat).	This means that errors made in journals are much less likely to be discovered before the entry is made.
Access to the general ledger is given to under-qualified staff.	Pat is the HR director making it unlikely that this individual has a sound understanding of accounting issues.
	Specifically, it is unlikely that the change to the rules for non-current assets could made correctly by someone without a thorough grasp of accounting rules.
	Errors could be made, deliberately or otherwise, in a crucial accounting document.
General ledger accounts can be created without authorisation.	Irregular or transactions could be hidden more easily in accounts created for the purpose.
A change to an accounting policy has been made without approval or indeed consultation.	Accounting policies must be consistently applied and appropriate for the business. If changed, then adjustments may be required in comparative figures and an explanation of the reason for the change included in the financial statements.
The friendship between Yoshika and Ping could undermine the controls within the business. There is evidence of this already as Yoshika is not asking for sight of journals from Ping due to a "trusting" environment that exists between them.	Journals which are wrong, or for inappropriate purposes, will lead to misstatements in the annual financial statements. This may lead users to make inappropriate decisions based upon that information.

41 INVENTORY PURCHASES

(i) Identify TWO types of fraud that may occur in the above situation. (2 marks)

(ii) Describe TWO circumstances that may allow each type of fraud identified to occur.

Type of fraud	Circumstances
Misappropriation of assets – physical	Theft of cash from petty cash tin/unauthorised expenditure as there is no formal authorisation recording process for petty cash taken out of the tin. Goods ordered for personal use resulting from: • goods not being checked to order and GRN on arrival, or • no order numbers/lack of controls for placing orders. Theft of inventory before it is recorded as a result of goods being left unattended in warehouse.
Misappropriation of financial statements – false accounting	Incorrect recording of trade payables as there is: • no segregation of duties within the purchase ledger, or • no authorisation of payments Incorrect recording of invoices/payments as there is no segregation of duties for checking and posting invoices, statements and payments. Unsubstantiated credit note claims recorded in the purchase ledger as there is no formal control or authorisation of goods returns or requests for credit notes.

42   INVENTORY PURCHASES

(i)   **Identify THREE potential risks in the system outlined above.**

(ii)   **Identify the potential implication of each risk identified.**

(iii) **Recommend an appropriate safeguard to minimise each risk.**

Potential risk	Potential implication	Safeguard to minimise risk
Collusion with supplier	Loss of inventory as goods are delivered to home address	Orders to be placed by a member of staff with no connection to the supplier OR Orders to a connected supplier are approved by a director
Reputational damage: poor quality cheap goods	Need to refund customers for poor quality goods	Review material wastage, returns and quality. Seek alternative supplier if necessary
May not be best price as no alternatives considered	Decreased profit, or Costs too high	Obtain more than one quote
Reputational damage: ethical impact of supply chain	Customers stop buying	Seek alternative, more ethically sound supplier

43 NON-CURRENT ASSETS

(i) **Identify THREE weaknesses in the system for the accurate recording of non-current assets outlined above.**

> **Only three required**
>
> - No segregation of duties: invoices processed and paid by same person
> - Invoice not matched to goods received note (GRN) or purchase order (PO)
> - Managers authorise assets for own department, with no apparent reference to budget or cashflow
> - Authorisation limit is high
> - Non-current asset register maintained and assets checked and adjusted by same person
> - Non-current asset calculations (depreciation, profit or loss on disposal) are not checked and may not be accurate

(ii) **Evaluate the impact that each of the weaknesses described in part (i) could have on the organisation.**

> - Fictitious suppliers may be paid as no supporting paper work is sent to accounts department which may cause cashflow issues, as well as the recording of non-existent assets
> - Assets delivered to departmental managers homes may not be discovered or may be a delay, costly for the business and may cause cash flow issues
> - Cashflow issues could arise where a series of uncoordinated, unbudgeted purchases are made, all authorised by different managers
> - Non-current assets may be incorrectly recorded in financial statements as a result of very few checks completed throughout the financial year
> - Financial statements will show an incorrect figure for non-current assets
> - Disposal of non-current assets may be incorrectly recorded – cost, depreciation, profit or loss on disposal. Financial statements will show an incorrect figure for non-current assets
> - Additions of non-current assets may be incorrectly recorded in the asset register, items missing or incorrect value, records will not reflect the actual assets held by the company
> - Potential loss of or identification of unused non-current assets will not be identified for some time
> - Incorrect depreciation methods or calculations used and will result in an incorrect profit figure being shown

UNDERSTAND THE IMPACT OF TECHNOLOGY ON ACCOUNTING SYSTEMS

44 NON-FINANCE PROFESSIONALS

Complete the following statements by selecting the correct option for each of the gaps below.

The best way to present financial data to non-finance professionals within your organisation is through a <<GAP 1 >>. You should consider the user's needs: determine what they need to see and then aim to <<GAP 2>>.

In order to check that the information you are presenting is in a suitable format for users to understand and interpret during the presentation, it is useful to <<GAP 3>>. You should then ensure that someone with limited technical knowledge can give you <<GAP 4>>.

Gap 1	✓
data dashboard	✓
pivot table	

Gap 2	✓
add interactive graphics	
eliminate clutter and distraction	✓

Gap 3	✓
check that you have given a definition for all the technical terms	
show it to someone who hasn't seen it before	✓

Gap 4	✓
a summary of the information contained within the presentation	✓
definitions for all the technical terms included in the presentation	

45 PASSWORDS

You have been asked to set up a new system of passwords for Healthyou's accounting system.

Which TWO of the following would reduce the effectiveness of passwords?

	✓
Requirement that passwords are changed every two weeks	
Users are allowed to choose their own passwords	✓
Automatic lock-out after 3 failed attempts to access system	
Making the sharing of passwords a disciplinary offence	
Displaying the password on the screen when entered	✓

46 MACHINE LEARNING

Identify whether the following statements about machine learning are true or false.

	True	False
Machine learning is a useful audit tool.	✓	
Machine learning cannot support multi-dimensional or multi-variety data.		✓
The use of machine learning to code raw data will improve the accuracy of the reports produced.	✓	
Machine learning does not enable continuous improvement.		✓
Humans do not need to be involved in decisions made using machine learning.		✓
Machine learning predictive models can be used to forecast revenue.	✓	

47 DATA ANALYTICS

Identify the relevant component required as part of the calculation for each of the following performance indicators

The reliance on algorithmic predictions when using data analytics to analyse a wide selection of data is a cause for...	Gap 1	...particularly if the outcome is then considered...	Gap 2

Gap 1	✓
accuracy concerns,	
ethical concerns,	✓

Gap 2	✓
biased and unfair.	✓
inaccurate and may be misleading.	

48 INFORMATION

The provision of information in a more appealing and understandable manner is often referred to as what?

	✓
Artificial Intelligence	
Cloud computing	
Data visualisation	✓
Data simplification	

49 SOCIAL MEDIA

Which of the 4 Vs of big data may be causing this problem?

	✓
Volume	
Variety	
Velocity	
Veracity	✓

50 WORKING FROM HOME

Identify which of the following are required for the security of finance data stored on your company laptop when working from home.

Statement	Required ✓	Not required ✓
Lock your screen if leaving your laptop unattended.		✓
Ensure data is stored on an encrypted hard drive.	✓	
Ensure access to USB ports has been restricted.	✓	

51 DATA VISUALISATION

Which of the following is a benefit of data visualisation for the finance function?

	✓
Weekly or monthly reporting will be produced on time	
Improved data security	
Improved fraud detection	
Improved insight and understanding	✓

52 CLOUD COMPUTING

Which of the following is a disadvantage of cloud computing?

	✓
Increased flexibility to working arrangements	
More reliance on third party suppliers	✓
Access to continually up to date software	
Easier integration of systems	

RECOMMEND IMPROVEMENTS TO ACCOUNTING SYSTEMS

CHANGES TO THE ACCOUNTING SYSTEM

53   SWOT ANALYSIS

What is a SWOT analysis?

	✓
It is a management method whereby an organization can assess major external factors that influence its operation in order to become more competitive in the market.	
It is an analysis framework that matches an organisation's goals, programmes and capacities to the environment in which it operates.	✓
It is a framework or tool used to analyse and monitor the macro-environmental factors that may have a profound impact on an organisation's performance.	

54   PESTLE ANALYSIS

What is a PESTLE analysis?

	✓
It is a management method whereby an organization can assess major external factors that influence its operation in order to become more competitive in the market.	
It is an analysis framework that matches an organisation's goals, programmes and capacities to the environment in which it operates.	
It is a framework or tool used to analyse and monitor the macro-environmental factors that may have a profound impact on an organisation's performance.	✓

55   PEST ANALYSIS

What is a PEST analysis?

	✓
It is a management method whereby an organization can assess major external factors that influence its operation in order to become more competitive in the market.	✓
It is an analysis framework that matches an organisation's goals, programmes and capacities to the environment in which it operates.	
It is a framework or tool used to analyse and monitor the macro-environmental factors that may have a profound impact on an organisation's performance.	

THE EFFECTS OF CHANGES ON USERS OF THE SYSTEM

56 CHANGEOVER

Which TWO of the following controls can mitigate the risk of system failure during direct changeover?

	✓
Training	
Testing	✓
Check digits	
System documentation	
Data backup	✓

57 INFORMATION SYSTEM CONTROLS

Identify the correct category for the following controls.

	Security ✓	Integrity ✓
Locked doors	✓	
Fire alarms	✓	
Passwords	✓	
Authorisation of data entry		✓
Batch totals		✓
Check digits		✓
Reconciliation		✓
CCTV	✓	

58 SALES ORDER PROCESSING

Complete a SWOT analysis for the procedures outlined above.

(i)   Identify ONE strength, ONE weakness, ONE opportunity to improve the procedures, and ONE threat to the effectiveness in the procedures outlined above.

(ii)   Explain how the strength benefits the organisation.

(iii)   Describe the potential damage this weakness could cause the organisation and a potential remedy.

(iv)   For the opportunity, explain how the procedure should be changed and how this would benefit the organisation

(v)   Explain how the threat could damage the organisation and an action that could reduce the risk.

(i) Strength Able to maintain up to date inventory records OR Easy for all customers to place orders	**(ii) Benefit** Customers will be able to place orders for available stock only, reduces waiting times and frustration of unknown waiting times for items that are out of stock
(i) Weakness Initial credit limit set and not updated quickly	**(iii) Damage** new customers may exceed their credit limit, which may increase bad debt new customers may not be able to place orders for the full amount of goods they need so may lose potential new customers delay in updating credit limit and chasing debt may lead to bad debts occurring **Remedy** Immediate update to credit limits Cash on delivery until credit checks are done
(i) Opportunity Improve the initial credit limit setting procedure, e.g. perform as a background website check when customers are placing an order	**(iv) Change** Introduce the facility for an initial online credit check to be performed before giving the initial credit limit. **Benefit** Would reduce bad debts Customers with good credit would be able to place larger orders

(i) **Threat**	(v) **Damage**
Adverse market reaction to bespoke products	May result in reputational damage Loss of customers to competitors **Action** Research current and potential customers to see if there is an appetite for bespoke products.

59 COST-BENEFIT ANALYSIS

Identify the appropriate category for each of the following statements.

Statement	Social ✓	Environmental ✓	Corporate ✓
Ability to recycle waste materials.		✓	
Reduced inventory levels resulting in reduced storage costs.			✓
Automation of production resulting in redundancies.	✓		
Change of delivery method to use electric vehicles.		✓	
Improved efficiencies following training staff resulting in cost savings.			✓

60 PESTLE

Identify the appropriate category for each statement from the PESTLE analysis findings.

Statement	Political ✓	Economical ✓	Social ✓	Technological ✓	Legal ✓	Environmental ✓
Initiative to reduce carbon footprint.						✓
Trade uncertainties in SMEs as result of changing legislation.					✓	
Changes due to Government legislation such as digital tax reporting.	✓					
Increased automation resulting in redundant admin tasks.		✓				
Investment in low energy products.						✓

Section 4

MOCK ASSESSMENT QUESTIONS

Scenario

The tasks in this assessment are all based on the scenario of Silversmith Ltd (Silversmith).

Silversmith started life as an independent jewellery manufacturer and retailer, and has grown significantly since first starting.

Following this period of rapid expansion, Silversmith have asked you, Safiya Bartelli, an Accounting Technician, to review the processes of the company and identify weaknesses in the internal controls that may have occurred due to the recent growth of the company.

Company background

History

Silversmith is a private limited company based in Harrogate which produces and distributes a range of silver jewellery.

The business began twelve years ago when Farah Silver started making silver earrings as a hobby. Farah was so successful that she decided to start a business, by obtaining premises and manufacturing an expanded range of jewellery.

She was joined by her cousin, Ben Smith, who had recently completed a Masters in Business Administration. Ben assumed responsibility for the administration of the business, allowing Farah to design and produce her own range of silver jewellery.

Farah and Ben decided to form Silversmith. They initially rented a large studio on an industrial estate in Harrogate, before expanding into a larger factory unit and warehouse on the same estate.

Recent developments

Silversmith has expanded rapidly over the last three years, through intense marketing activities and a successful online presence on popular social media sites. The company now employs several staff and has opened additional warehouses in Glasgow and Southampton.

In the last few months, the company has opened a second factory on its site in Southampton.

Silversmith has signed supply contracts with various high street retailers as well as continuing to supply independent stores. Retail customers are able to purchase direct from a factory shop at the Harrogate site.

Silversmith has also opened a number of small workshops in rented premises in a number of towns. These workshops, branded as Silversmith Studio, provide activity days where members of the public can make their own jewellery, as well as providing local retail outlets.

Ben has researched developments in the jewellery market and feels that Silversmith would be able to expand more quickly if it expanded its range beyond silver jewellery to include other forms of jewellery and giftware.

Resources

On 31 December 20X7, Silversmith had 72 employees.

Department	Number of staff
Manufacturing	15
Storage and distribution	26
Studio	10
Sales and Marketing	8
Administration	8
Design and development	5

Most of the above employees are based at the Harrogate site, which is where the bulk of goods are produced. However, this site is now operating at capacity, so any additional production has been switched to Southampton.

This has led to increased costs for the company, so it is looking at alternative production processes to reduce costs, possibly including outsourcing.

Staff

Some of Silversmith's key personnel are listed below:

Managing Director	Farah Silver
Operations Director	Ben Smith
Finance Director	Emma Raducanu
Financial Controller	Leylah Fernandez
Credit Controller	Brian Jones
Accounts Payable Clerk	Joanne Harten
Accounts Receivable Clerk	Josh Pugh
General Accounts Clerk and Cashier	Jasmine Taylor
Payroll Clerk	Gloria Jones
Production Manager	Geva Mentor
Sales and Marketing Manager	Sanjay Patel
Warehousing Manager	Lee Johnson
Transport Manager	Karla Pretorius

Sustainability

The company has launched a comprehensive training programme for all employees, allowing it to ensure high standards of employee satisfaction, as well as workplace safety and productivity.

Environmentally, Silversmith has made a 'zero-carbon' pledge to reduce carbon emissions (with an aim to becoming 'carbon negative'). It is also keen to cut wastage with a view to financial savings. So far, this has included:

- reduced amounts of packaging for items delivered to customers

- amending the supplier approval process to focus on sustainability, through good working practices and fair pay

- increased levels of recycling

- automatic lighting via a sensor system

TASK 1 (25 MARKS)

This task is about the purpose, structure and organisation of the accounting function.

You have been asked to review and develop a policy on ethics and sustainability for implementation over the next few years.

(a) (i) **Identify whether each of the following would be a way to improve ethics and sustainability.**

Statement	Would improve ✓	Would not improve ✓
Replace current plastic packaging with recyclable cardboard.		
Allowing a greater number of employees to park their cars on-site by re-painting the marked parking bays in the carpark.		
Switching production of jewellery abroad to improve profitability.		

(3 marks)

You are training Eliana, a new junior accountant who is joining your team. You feel that in order to provide the best training to Eliana, it is important that she understands organisational structure. Eliana has told you that she has recently studied the differences between tall and flat organisational structures.

(a) (ii) **Identify whether the following statements about a flat organisational structure are true or false.**

Statement	True ✓	False ✓
A flat organisation has a long scalar chain.		
A flat organisation has fewer levels of management than a tall organisation.		
A flat organisation has a narrow span of control.		
A flat organisation is less expensive than a tall organisation.		

(4 marks)

Eliana has been learning about performance indicators as part of her training. She's still a little unsure about some of the calculations, so has asked you to identify what information from the financial statements is needed to calculate certain performance indicators.

(a)   (iii)   Identify the relevant component required as part of the calculation for each of the following performance indicators.

Return on capital employed	Gap 1
Gearing	Gap 2
Operating profit margin	Gap 3
Trade payables collection period	Gap 4

Gap 1	✓
Gross profit	
Operating profit	
Non-current assets	
Non-current liabilities	

Gap 2	✓
Equity	
Finance costs	
Operating profit	
Non-current assets	

Gap 3	✓
Equity	
Trade receivables	
Revenue	
Cost of sales	

Gap 4	✓
Trade receivables	
Revenue	
Cost of sales	
Total current assets	

(4 marks)

In an effort to improve employees' work-life balance by reducing commuting time Silversmith have started to allow non-production staff to work from home. Staff still need to ensure that appropriate data is maintained securely, with no breach of data security regulations. To assist in this process, Silversmith uses cloud accounting.

(b)   (i)   Identify whether the following statements relating to cloud accounting are true or false.

Statement	True ✓	False ✓
Remote working using cloud accounting will improve document accessibility		
The use of cloud accounting will lead to increased hardware costs.		
The use of cloud accounting will mean that businesses are more likely to lose data.		
The use of cloud accounting means that data is always secure.		

(4 marks)

You have been working with Eliana to review Silversmith's data and operational security policy. Eliana has identified the following situations but is unsure which type of risk they represent.

(b) (ii) Identify the correct risk for each statement below.

Statement	Risk
Farah had asked Gloria to send her the details of management salaries, but Gloria accidentally sent a group email to all Silversmith employees.	
During the recent hot weather, Henry, the office assistant, unplugged the main server in order to plug in a fan.	
Eliana discovered that Lee, the Warehousing Manager, has deactivated his antivirus software as it makes his laptop too slow.	
Eliana received an email that was apparently from a delivery service, telling her that they had tried unsuccessfully to deliver her parcel, and that she needed to click on a link to arrange re-delivery. Eliana did not think that she had ordered anything.	

Options
Loss of data
Data breach
Unauthorised remote access
Phishing

(4 marks)

As the levels of Silversmith's business have grown over the years, the volume of data processed has also significantly increased. The distribution of data at Silversmith's disposal depends on the level of management, each needing different levels of data. Eliana is unsure about these management levels and the appropriate type of data for each. You have produced a training document to assist Eliana, which includes a brief description of the different levels of management and the information that each level will use.

(c)   (i)   Identify the information level corresponding to the described management roles within Silversmith.

Management role	
Farah Silver chairs any board meetings where Silversmith's long-term plans are discussed. The Sales and Marketing and Production Managers report their issues to Farah periodically at these meetings.	Gap 1
Lee Johnson is responsible for the day-to-day running of the Harrogate warehouse.	Gap 2
Geva Mentor is responsible for the assessment of performance and allocation of production resources to all locations.	Gap 3

Gap options	Gap No.
Operational level	
Tactical level	
Strategic level	

(3 marks)

(c) **(ii)** Identify the correct information option that corresponds with the described information available within Silversmith

Data available	
Weekly production reports and staff shift pattern planner reports.	Gap 1
Annual stamping-machine utilisation percentage reports, and budget versus actual outputs per production unit.	Gap 2
Five-year profit or loss and cash flow forecasts, used to plan the timing of investments in machinery and potential new locations for Silversmith Studios.	Gap 3

Gap options	Gap No.
Tactical information	
Strategic information	
Operational information	

(3 marks)

TASK 2 (25 MARKS)

This task is about the types of fraud in the workplace combined with ways in which it can be detected and prevented.

In addition to its two manufacturing locations, Silversmith has many Silversmith Studios across the country, and three warehouses in Harrogate, Glasgow and Southampton. Due to the number of locations it is not possible for the Senior Management team to attend all the inventory counts, but local management have clear counting instructions and report back to head office.

Silversmith's warehouses are operational 24 hours a day, receiving raw materials from suppliers and despatching them to Silversmith's factories, as well as receiving finished goods from the factories before despatching them to customers and Studios.

The company uses a courier service for all its outward deliveries. Due to low staffing levels, the couriers load the inventory onto their vehicles themselves. When the courier arrives for a collection, the warehouse receptionist passes them the goods despatch notes (GDNs) and directs them to the appropriate area of the warehouse.

To ensure that inventory records are up-to-date, local staff perform regular inventory counts, and then make any necessary adjustments to the inventory records.

(a)   Complete the following statement by selecting the correct options to complete the gaps below.

The above may result in the occurrence of ___GAP 1___ fraud, that occur as a result of ___GAP2__

In order to address this risk Silversmith need to implement ___GAP 3___ as soon as possible. This will ensure that the impact on ___GAP 4___ is minimised.

Gap 1	✓
misstatement of financial statements	
e-crime	
misappropriation of assets	

Gap 2	✓
lack of written instruction	
lack of a risk matrix	
lack of controls	

Gap 3	✓
segregation of duties	
written instructions	
a series of physical controls	

Gap 4	✓
assets	
income	
liabilities	

(4 marks)

Ben Smith, Operations Director, observed that unfavourable discrepancies have been reported between budgeted and actual income, cash and inventory levels from the Silversmith Studios section of the business. Ben has conducted a review into the processes within the Silversmith Studios and discovered the following issues:

Customers can order jewellery through the Silversmith website for 'click and collect' at their local Silversmith Studio. The studios store these packages in a small, unlocked storeroom at the back of the studio. Once customers have provided staff with a reference number for their order, the customers collect their package from the storeroom, and then return to the counter, where a member of staff confirms that the order number on the package matches the customer's order number.

Silversmith Studio retail customers pay with cash or card when buying jewellery. Each studio has an online till system to record sales and payments and issue refunds, together with a machine for card payments. Daily reconciliations of the till records compared to the cash takings and card receipts from machines are performed by the studio manager once the studio has shut. The studios employ few staff and often studio managers serve customers when the studios are busy. The studios often have evening workshops, finishing late in the evening, so studio managers will sometimes take cash takings home before banking the next day.

Customers can book workshops online via the Silversmith website or contact their local studio directly. Each workshop is run by a local freelance silversmith and focuses on a single type of jewellery, either earrings, rings, bracelets or necklaces. The studio can hold up to eight participants although no record is kept of attendees or the type of jewellery produced.

Deliveries of jewellery for resale and raw materials for the workshops are signed for by the studio managers. Inventory counts for each studio should be carried out on the last day of the month, after the studio has closed for the day. The studio managers are responsible for the count and then provide a monthly inventory report to head office. It has been reported that a number of studio managers actually perform the counts during the day to avoid staying late.

(b) **(i)** **Identify FOUR weakness in the system that may result in fraud occurring. (4 marks)**

(b) **(ii)** **Recommend an internal control for EACH weakness, giving a reason why it would help to prevent fraud.** **(8 marks)**

Weakness that may result in fraud	Internal control to help prevent fraud and reason

During your AAT studies, you learned about recording fraud risk on a fraud matrix. You have discovered a number of potential areas where fraud could arise. You must complete a fraud matrix to assess the potential risks. The issues are described in the table below.

(c) **Identify the appropriate rating for each of the situations given below.**

Situation
In the early days of the business, Farah and Ben handled their own bookkeeping requirements and a local accountancy firm in Harrogate prepared the accounts. As the business grew it became necessary to adapt, first by using the local firm's bookkeeping service, and then by creating Silversmith's own accounts department. This has been operating for a number of years and staff turnover is low. All staff in the department are either professionally qualified or studying towards a professional qualification. The business uses a well-established accounting software package, which is regularly reviewed and updated.
Silversmith are reviewing the payroll system and discover that there is a high turnover of staff, particularly in the Silversmith Studio sites. Silversmith Studio's staffing levels fluctuate between peak and off-peak seasons. As a result, many temporary staff are hired during peak times such as Christmas, and, due to time constraints, it is not always possible to take up formal employment references prior to employing these staff. A number of these staff are paid in cash on a self-employed basis.
Silversmith is proud of its approach to training, and initially provided sufficient training to provide cover for holidays and sickness. As the business has become more cost-conscious, it has been decided to only train one person for each role.

Options

5 – Very high
3 – Medium
1 – Very low

(3 marks)

You have discussed the system of ordering and accepting goods into the Glasgow warehouse with Lee Johnson, the Warehousing Manager. You have identified the following risks with this system:

- **Unauthorised orders being placed informally over the phone**

  Silversmith have an approved suppliers list, which is reviewed annually. As a result, goods can only be ordered from these suppliers, although they will accept telephone orders with no purchase order number.

- **Risk of accepting unauthorised, inaccurate or damaged deliveries**

  Goods are often delivered overnight, and are unloaded into a secure storage area adjacent to the warehouse. The storage area has keycode access and the delivery drivers use the code when unloading goods. At the start of the working day, the goods are checked for quantity and damage, before being transferred into the warehouse. Lee admits that deliveries often appear to be short or damaged.

- **Theft of goods due to couriers' keycode access to storage area**

  Goods are also collected overnight. Warehouse staff move goods for collection from the warehouse into the secure storage area during the day. The delivery notes are attached to the goods, and couriers access them overnight, using the keycode access.

(d) **Outline how you can MONITOR, REVIEW and REPORT on ONE of the risks within the system above.** **(6 marks)**

TASK 3 (10 MARKS)

This task is about the effectiveness of internal controls.

Jasmine Taylor, General Accounts Clerk and Cashier, has approached you for some advice. She has suggested some internal controls, but wants to check that she fully understands what internal controls are and how they work. Jasmine has therefore asked you to check that her suggested controls are suitable for the purpose that she has identified, as she knows that you have recently completed your studies.

(a) **Identify whether the following internal controls are suitable for the purpose given.**

Internal control	Purpose	Is the internal control suitable? ✓
Ensuring pre-employment checks are completed for all new staff members prior to employment, and payments can only be made to staff on the payroll.	Compliance	Yes ☐ No ☐
All deliveries received checked to supplier delivery note, then checked against purchase order. Delivery note signed to acknowledge both checks.	Ensure quality internal and external reporting	Yes ☐ No ☐
Complete monthly supplier statement reconciliations, reviewed and signed by responsible person.	Safeguard assets	Yes ☐ No ☐
Segregation of duties between authorisation and payment of supplier invoices	Prevent and detect fraud	Yes ☐ No ☐

(4 marks)

Following recent negative press surrounding UK textile factories using cheap labour, Farah and Ben are keen to publicise Silversmith's reputation for ethical behaviour. A review of the finance department identified that some of the systems in place do not promote ethical behaviours.

The following improvements to the system have been suggested to address this.

(b) **Identify which of the following would promote ethical behaviours within an organisation.**

Improvement	Promote ✓	Would not promote ✓
Working practices of all suppliers to be assessed prior to acceptance onto the approved supplier list.		
The purchasing policy permits the payment of bribes in countries where this is necessary to secure supply contracts.		
Ensure that all new starters sign non-disclosure agreements preventing staff from posting negative comments about Silversmith on social media.		
In order to retain the services of senior managers, their annual bonuses are guaranteed.		
Every staff member has the ability to use two fully-paid days per annum to perform voluntary work, e.g. with a local charity		
Recruitment policies should ensure that vacancy shortlisting is carried out 'blind', i.e. without revealing any of the candidate's personal details.		

(6 marks)

TASK 4 (15 MARKS)

This task is about the monitoring of accounting systems and how they work in practice.

The current systems for high street retail outlet customers to place orders and for sales to be recorded are:

- orders are placed using Silversmith's website (using customer log-ins).

- all orders are processed by the sales department who do not require an order number.

- all customers are given a 30-day credit account to encourage repeat business.

- sales orders are passed to the supervisor of the nearest warehouse (Harrogate, Glasgow or Southampton) where they are packed ready for collection.

- most orders are collected by a national courier, but some nearby customers prefer to collect their own goods to save time and delivery costs.

- on collection, couriers sign a goods despatched note (GDN) which is retained by the local warehouse supervisors to enable them to resolve any customer queries in respect of damage or shortage.

- proofs of delivery (including mobile device photos where necessary) are provided by the courier to the warehouse supervisor, who stores them at the warehouse for reference. Any returned goods are placed back into the warehouse.

- no GDN or proof of delivery is obtained for those local customers who collect in person.

- invoices are prepared by the accounts department and issued by the sales department once the goods are despatched. Josh Pugh, the Accounts Receivable Clerk, enters the invoices into the accounting system.

- at the end of each month Josh sends out customer statements.

- Josh opens the post each morning and banks any cheques received. Josh also reviews the online banking system for any direct credits from customers. Josh then enters the receipts into the accounting system, and to the relevant customer accounts.

(a) Analyse the potential deficiencies in the system outlined above, together with their cause AND impact. **(10 marks)**

Emma Raducanu, Finance Director, decided that a thorough review of the payroll system is needed. The last time a similar review occurred was 24 months ago, and any changes necessary have since been implemented. A number of the staff have said that there is little point in such a review, as most of the staff are the same, and the same controls are still in place.

(b) **Identify the correct response to complete the gaps below.**

The payroll department's internal controls need to be reviewed to ensure that	Gap 1	which may have occurred because...	Gap 2

Gap 1	✓
the internal control objectives are not irrelevant	
there are no dummy employees	

Gap 2	✓
of the low staff turnover.	
of changes in technology.	

(2 marks)

(c) **Identify whether the following statements are true or false.**

Statement	True ✓	False ✓
If management are able to override controls, this shows a weak control environment		
Lack of segregation of duties will always lead to fraud.		
The bank reconciliation acts as a type of internal control.		

(3 marks)

TASK 5

This task is about the analysis of internal controls with recommendations to improve whilst considering the impact on users.

For this task, you are Jasmine Taylor, General Accounts Clerk and Cashier.

Silversmith is looking to continue with the recent rapid expansion and Farah Silver (Managing Director) agrees with Ben Smith (Operations Director) that the best route to achieve this is through expanding their product range into other forms of jewellery and giftware.

The current system for costing a new jewellery product is a manual system. The limited range of jewellery currently produced has meant that up to now this manual system has been adequate. However, Emma Raducanu, the Finance Director, believes that there are increased risks of costing errors when using manual costings for an expanding range of products, especially given that Silversmith have never produced some of these items before.

Emma has commissioned research that identified the most suitable costing system for jewellery and giftware as one called JAGS. The cost of this research was £2,800.

You would need to attend a three-day training course at a cost of £500 per day. The Production Manager, Geva Mentor, would also need to attend the same course, along with two members of the production team.

The JAGS system would require new hardware to run it, so Farah has decided to upgrade all Silversmith's hardware to ensure maximum capacity and integration. As a result, there will be a cost of £124,000 per annum for the hardware. The annual licence fee for the software amounts to £14,000.

On reviewing the potential benefits of the new system you have identified that less overtime will be needed by both production and finance staff, with monthly management reports produced more quickly. The annual saving in overtime is likely to amount to £18,000.

A group of current high street retailer customers were enthusiastic when shown the new range of products. Based on their response, Sanjay Patel, Sales and Marketing Manager, believes that these new products are likely to generate additional annual profit of £220,000, which he says is a conservative estimate.

(a) **(i)** **Complete a financial cost-benefit analysis for the above proposal.**

Costs	£
Benefits	£
(Net Cost)/Benefit (£)	

(6 marks)

(a) (ii) Identify SIX non-financial factors that should be taken into account as part of the cost benefit analysis.

(6 marks)

(a) (iii) Recommend, with TWO reasons, whether or not the proposed investment should be made.

(3 marks)

As an additional task, and in preparation for the potential changes needed if the new system is introduced, you have also been looking at benefits of implementing new systems.

(b) **(i)** **Identify which FOUR of the following would be considered to be intangible benefits of changing the information system.**

Benefit	✓
Improved customer service	
Quicker decision-making	
Savings in maintenance costs	
More time for strategic planning	
Reduced inventory levels	
Competitive advantage though lower costs	
Reduced staff overtime	
Better understanding of customer needs	

(4 marks)

(b) **(ii)** **Identify whether the following characteristics are associated with switching directly from the old system to a new system.**

Characteristic	Associated ✓	Not Associated ✓
More expensive than alternative methods of implementation		
The business need not ensure that the new system is working perfectly before switching		
Eases the processing workload		
Increases risk of an unsuccessful changeover compared to other methods		
Increases confidence in results from the new system		
Can sometimes represent the only possible solution		

(6 marks)

Section 5

ANSWERS TO MOCK ASSESSMENT QUESTIONS

TASK 1 (25 MARKS)

(a) **(i)** Identify whether each of the following would be a way to improve ethics and sustainability.

Statement	Would improve ✓	Would not improve ✓
Replace current plastic packaging with recyclable cardboard.	✓	
Allowing a greater number of employees to park their cars on-site by re-painting the marked parking bays in the carpark.		✓
Switching production of jewellery abroad to improve profitability.		✓

(3 marks)

(a) **(ii)** Identify whether the following statements about a flat organisational structure are true or false.

Statement	True ✓	False ✓
A flat organisation has a long scalar chain.		✓
A flat organisation has fewer levels of management than a tall organisation.	✓	
A flat organisation has a narrow span of control.		✓
A flat organisation is less expensive than a tall organisation.	✓	

(4 marks)

(a) **(iii)** **Identify the relevant component required as part of the calculation for each of the following performance indicators.**

Return on capital employed	Gap 1
Gearing	Gap 2
Operating profit margin	Gap 3
Trade payables collection period	Gap 4

Gap 1	✓
Gross profit	
Operating profit	✓
Non-current assets	
Non-current liabilities	

Gap 2	✓
Equity	✓
Finance costs	
Operating profit	
Non-current assets	

Gap 3	✓
Equity	
Trade receivables	
Revenue	✓
Cost of sales	

Gap 4	✓
Trade receivables	
Revenue	
Cost of sales	✓
Total current assets	

(4 marks)

(b) **(i)** **Identify whether the following statements relating to cloud accounting are true or false.**

Statement	True ✓	False ✓
Remote working using cloud accounting will improve document accessibility	✓	
The use of cloud accounting will lead to increased hardware costs.		✓
The use of cloud accounting will mean that businesses are more likely to lose data.		✓
The use of cloud accounting means that data is always secure.		✓

(4 marks)

(b)   (ii)   Identify the correct risk for each statement below.

Statement	Risk
Farah had asked Gloria to send her the details of management salaries, but Gloria accidentally sent a group email to all Silversmith employees.	Data breach
During the recent hot weather, Henry, the office assistant, unplugged the main server in order to plug in a fan.	Loss of data
Eliana discovered that Lee, the Warehousing Manager, has deactivated his antivirus software as it makes his laptop too slow.	Unauthorised remote access
Eliana received an email that was apparently from a delivery service, telling her that they had tried unsuccessfully to deliver her parcel, and that she needed to click on a link to arrange re-delivery. Eliana did not think that she had ordered anything.	Phishing

Options
Loss of data
Data breach
Unauthorised remote access
Phishing

(4 marks)

(c)   (i)   Identify the information level corresponding to the described management roles within Silversmith.

Management role	
Farah Silver chairs any board meetings where Silversmith's long-term plans are discussed. The Sales and Marketing and Production Managers report their issues to Farah periodically at these meetings.	Gap 1
Lee Johnson is responsible for the day-to-day running of the Harrogate warehouse.	Gap 2
Geva Mentor is responsible for the assessment of performance and allocation of production resources to all locations.	Gap 3

Gap options	No.
Operational level	Gap 2
Tactical level	Gap 3
Strategic level	Gap 1

(3 marks)

(c)   (ii)   Identify the correct information option that corresponds with the described information available within Silversmith

Data available	
Weekly production reports and staff shift pattern planner reports.	Gap 1
Annual stamping-machine utilisation percentage reports, and budget versus actual outputs per production unit.	Gap 2
Five-year profit or loss and cash flow forecasts, used to plan the timing of investments in machinery and potential new locations for Silversmith Studios.	Gap 3

Gap options	No.
Tactical information	Gap 2
Strategic information	Gap 3
Operational information	Gap 1

(3 marks)

TASK 2 (25 MARKS)

(a) **Complete the following statement by selecting the correct options to complete the gaps below.**

The above may result in the occurrence of ___GAP 1___ fraud, that occur as a result of ___GAP2__

In order to address this risk Silversmith need to implement ___GAP 3___ as soon as possible. This will ensure that the impact on ___GAP 4___ is minimised.

Gap 1	✓
misstatement of financial statements	
e-crime	
misappropriation of assets	✓

Gap 2	✓
lack of written instruction	
lack of a risk matrix	
lack of controls	✓

Gap 3	✓
segregation of duties	
written instructions	
a series of physical controls	✓

Gap 4	✓
assets	✓
income	
liabilities	

(4 marks)

(b) (i) **Identify FOUR weakness in the system that may result in fraud occurring.**

(4 marks)

(b) (ii) **Recommend an internal control for EACH weakness, giving a reason why it would help to prevent fraud.** (8 marks)

Weakness that may result in fraud	Internal control to help prevent fraud and reason
Storeroom is unlocked (1)	Storeroom should be locked (1) to prevent unauthorised access (1)
Customers collect their own package (1)	Staff should collect package (1) to prevent customers stealing other packages and inventory (1)
Studio manager (SM) takes cash home (1)	Reconciled cash takings to be banked in night-safe (1) to prevent later manipulation by SM (1)

Cash sales to be discontinued, with card-only sales (1) to remove opportunity for loss of cash (1) |

Workshop run by freelance silversmith (FS) with: No record of attendees (1) or type of jewellery (1) could result in: misappropriated cash from unrecorded attendees (1) loss of inventory due to more raw material being used than needed, excess removed by FS (1)	All workshop attendees to book online (1) to prevent unregistered attendees paying cash direct to FS (1) Inventory used in workshops to be signed out by FS, specifying type of jewellery, to allow reconciliation by SM (1) to prevent excess being removed by FS (1) SM to review workshop details to verify number of attendees and type of jewellery (1) to prevent inventory theft (1)
No segregation of duties for inventory: SM signs for deliveries and performs inventory count (1)	Separate member of staff to perform count, countersigned by SM (1) to prevent misappropriation of inventory (1)

(c)   **Identify the appropriate rating for each of the situations given below.**

Rating	Situation
Option 1 1 – Very low	In the early days of the business, Farah and Ben handled their own bookkeeping requirements and a local accountancy firm in Harrogate prepared the accounts. As the business grew it became necessary to adapt, first by using the local firm's bookkeeping service, and then by creating Silversmith's own accounts department. This has been operating for a number of years and staff turnover is low. All staff in the department are either professionally qualified or studying towards a professional qualification. The business uses a well-established accounting software package, which is regularly reviewed and updated.
Option 2 5 – Very high	Silversmith are reviewing the payroll system and discover that there is a high turnover of staff, particularly in the Silversmith Studio sites. Silversmith Studio's staffing levels fluctuate between peak and off-peak seasons. As a result, many temporary staff are hired during peak times such as Christmas, and, due to time constraints, it is not always possible to take up formal employment references prior to employing these staff. A number of these staff are paid in cash on a self-employed basis.
Option 3 3 – Medium	Silversmith is proud of its approach to training, and initially provided sufficient training to provide cover for holidays and sickness. As the business has become more cost-conscious, it has been decided to only train one person for each role.

Options

5 – Very high
3 – Medium
1 – Very low

(3 marks)

(d)   Outline how you can MONITOR, REVIEW and REPORT on ONE of the risks within the system above.   **(6 marks)**

---

1 x mark for reference to any points below: max 6 marks for ONE risk

Risk – Unauthorised orders can be placed informally over the phone.

Monitor: max 2 marks

- set up authorised purchasers/buyers who are the only staff who can order goods from suppliers. This should enable monitoring of orders placed per staff member to help identify unusual purchasing practices. (1)

- management authorisation needed before any orders can be completed to ensure management are monitoring orders being placed. (1)

- check in the warehouse that orders being delivered have the appropriate level of authorisation by matching of goods received notes to management authorisation documents/POs before accepting deliveries. (1)

Review: max 2 marks

- periodic spot checks by management of samples of large invoices or purchase orders and trace to authorisation documents to ensure that authorisation controls are being followed. (1)

- investigate invoices for which there is no PO (1)

- internal audit /walk through test (1) to identify where the controls are not being followed and the areas that need additional controls (1)

- compare budgeted expenditure to actual expenditure to spot unusual variances (1)

- perform regular supplier statement reconciliations to highlight discrepancies between supplier's records and Silversmith's purchase ledger (1)

Report: max 2 marks

- invoice in accounts department matched to PO (1) and inconsistencies checked with supplier (1)

- produce table/chart (1) that shows potential differences between costs incurred and budgets.(1)

- produce analysis of monthly orders placed with no PO to highlight unusual activity (1)

OR

Risk – Risk of accepting unauthorised, inaccurate or damaged deliveries due to no system to check and record items received

Monitor: max 2 marks

- delivery quantities and line items matched to information on PO's and authorisation documents before acceptance at the warehouse (1) and inconsistencies checked with supplier (1)

- warehouse manager inspects condition of goods within warehouse for evidence of damaged items accepted (1)

- ensure deliveries are accepted and signed by more than 1 person and a manager (1)

- perform inventory counts to assess condition and numbers of inventory (1)

Review: max 2 marks

- internal audit /walk through test (1) to identify areas that need additional controls (1)
- review monthly inventory write off reports for unusual activity to identify levels of write off (could indicate damaged goods accepted) (1)

Report: max 2 marks

- produce table/chart (1) that shows monthly credit notes activity for evidence of unusual returns to quantify the problem (1)
- monthly report of write offs of inventory lines (1) or damaged goods discovered on the count (1)

OR

Risk – Theft of goods due to courier keycode access to storage area

Monitor: max 2 marks

when overnight despatches have occurred, perform daily inventory counts to assess expected quantities of inventory to actuals (1)

install CCTV covering warehouse overnight(1)

Review: max 2 marks

- internal audit /walk through test (1) to identify areas that need additional controls (1)
- review reports of unexpected incidences of stock-outs (1) to identify unexpected stock shortages and missing inventories (1)

Report: max 2 marks

- monthly report of under/over inventory line quantities (1) discovered on the count (1)
- produce table/chart (1) that shows potential differences, loss of inventory (1)

All three elements of the above must relate to a given risk.

TASK 3 (10 MARKS)

(a) Identify whether the following internal controls are suitable for the purpose given.

Internal control	Purpose	Is the internal control suitable? ✓	
Ensuring pre-employment checks are completed for all new staff members prior to employment, and payments can only be made to staff on the payroll.	Compliance	Yes	✓
		No	
All deliveries received checked to supplier delivery note, then checked against purchase order. Delivery note signed to acknowledge both checks.	Ensure quality internal and external reporting	Yes	
		No	✓
Complete monthly supplier statement reconciliations, reviewed and signed by responsible person.	Safeguard assets	Yes	
		No	✓
Segregation of duties between authorisation and payment of supplier invoices	Prevent and detect fraud	Yes	✓
		No	

(4 marks)

(b) **Identify which of the following would promote ethical behaviours within an organisation.**

Improvement	Promote ✓	Would not promote ✓
Working practices of all suppliers to be assessed prior to acceptance onto the approved supplier list.	✓	
The purchasing policy permits the payment of bribes in countries where this is necessary to secure supply contracts.		✓
Ensure that all new starters sign non-disclosure agreements preventing staff from posting negative comments about Silversmith on social media.		✓
In order to retain the services of senior managers, their annual bonuses are guaranteed.		✓
Every staff member has the ability to use two fully-paid days per annum to perform voluntary work, e.g. with a local charity	✓	
Recruitment policies should ensure that vacancy shortlisting is carried out 'blind', i.e. without revealing any of the candidate's personal details.	✓	

(6 marks)

TASK 4 (15 MARKS)

(a) Analyse the potential deficiencies in the system outlined above, together with their cause AND impact. (10 marks)

Deficiencies

- No customer order number
- Orders are not matched to invoices or delivery notes
- Credit given to potentially non-creditworthy customers
- No signed collection notes for local customers
- Accounts department do not have signed delivery proofs
- Potential for deliveries to be not be invoiced
- Accounts are not aware of returned or damaged goods
- Josh has full responsibility for recording of invoices, cash received and statements

Causes

- Lack of mandatory order numbers for all orders
- No credit checks performed before allowing credit
- Lack of formal procedure for collection of goods
- Lack of formal procedure to ensure that all orders are recorded and invoiced
- Lack of formal system for recording returns or damaged goods
- Lack of segregation of duties

Impact

- Orders may be sent incorrectly
- Invoices may be for the incorrect goods and/or amount
- Potential theft by employees – may create fake accounts as no credit checks done
- Potential theft by employees – may steal cash, then issue credit notes to cover theft
- Poor relationship with/loss of customers due to invoice/credit note disputes
- Unrecorded sales - orders/delivery/invoices all completed separately

Other relevant points may be considered.

(b) Identify the correct response to complete the gaps below.

The payroll department's internal controls need to be reviewed to ensure that	Gap 1	which may have occurred because…	Gap 2

Gap 1	✓	Gap 2	✓
the internal control objectives are not irrelevant	✓	of the low staff turnover.	
there are no dummy employees		of changes in technology.	✓

(2 marks)

(c)   Identify whether the following statements are true or false.

Statement	True ✓	False ✓
If management are able to override controls, this shows a weak control environment	✓	
Lack of segregation of duties will always lead to fraud.		✓
The bank reconciliation acts as a type of internal control.	✓	

(3 marks)

TASK 5 (25 MARKS)

(a) (i) **Complete a financial cost-benefit analysis for the above proposal.**

Costs	£
Hardware costs	124,000
Software costs	14,000
Training costs (4 people × 3 days × £500)	6,000
Benefits	**£**
Profit from new products	220,000
Overtime saving	18,000
(Net Cost)/Benefit (£)	Benefit £94,000

(6 marks)

(a) (ii) Identify SIX non-financial factors that should be taken into account as part of the cost benefit analysis.

1 x mark for reference to any points below: max 6 marks

Enhanced reputation of Silversmith as major supplier of broader range of jewellery and giftware.

Staff satisfaction at removal of the manual system.

Staff satisfaction at reduced working hours, improving work-life balance and reputation as an ethical employer.

Staff dissatisfaction at lack of overtime.

Speedier production of reports.

Faster decisions on whether to proceed with production of a new product.

Improvement in staff morale as they see increased investment levels.

Potential difficulties in switching to new system.

Time taken to use system efficiently (learning curve)

Other relevant points may earn marks.

(6 marks)

(a) (iii) Recommend, with TWO reasons, whether or not the proposed investment should be made.

1 x mark for recommendation: 2 marks for supporting explanation – max 3 marks

Recommendation:

Yes, the proposed investment should be made (OFR based on own calculations) because of reasons below (1)

Reasons:

Enhanced reputation (1)

Increased revenue (1)

Reduced overtime costs (1)

Cost-benefit analysis shows net benefit (1)

Improved speed of costing (1)

Improved speed of reporting (1)

Enhanced ethical reputation due to reduced working hours (1)

OR

Recommendation:

No, the proposed investment should not be made (OFR based on own calculations) because of reasons below (1)

Reasons:

Cost-benefit analysis shows net cost (OFR) (1)

Staff unrest – reduced overtime (1)

Staff unrest – fear of change (1)

Difficulty changing system (1)

Staff may not be able to use the new system (1)

(3 marks)

(b) (i) Identify which FOUR of the following would be considered to be intangible benefits of changing the information system.

Benefit	✓
Improved customer service	✓
Quicker decision-making	✓
Savings in maintenance costs	
More time for strategic planning	✓
Reduced inventory levels	
Competitive advantage though lower costs	
Reduced staff overtime	
Better understanding of customer needs	✓

(4 marks)

(b) (ii) Identify whether the following characteristics are associated with switching directly from the old system to a new system.

Characteristic	Associated ✓	Not Associated ✓
More expensive than alternative methods of implementation		✓
The business need not ensure that the new system is working perfectly before switching		✓
Eases the processing workload	✓	
Increases risk of an unsuccessful changeover compared to other methods	✓	
Increases confidence in results from the new system		✓
Can sometimes represent the only possible solution	✓	

(6 marks)